Hound Dog Days

One Dog and his Man

A Story of North Country Life
and Canine Contentment

Harry Pearson

ABACUS

First published in Great Britain in 2008 by Little, Brown
This paperback edition published in 2009 by Abacus

Copyright © Harry Pearson 2008

A CIP catalogue record for this book
is available from the British Library.

ISBN 978-0-349-12037-9

Typeset in Baskerville by M Rules
Printed and bound in Great Britain by
Clays Ltd, St Ives plc

Papers used by Abacus are natural, renewable and recyclable
products sourced from well-managed forests and certified
in accordance with the rules of the Forest Stewardship Council.

Mixed Sources
Product group from well-managed
forests and other controlled sources
www.fsc.org Cert no. SGS-COC-004081
FSC © 1996 Forest Stewardship Council

Preface

This is how my day begins. The squeak of a floorboard wakes me. The bedroom is in total darkness. No light comes through the westerly facing window. Not a shadow shows itself. I hear feet pattering across the wooden floor of the corridor. The noise stops, indicating not that the visitor has halted but that he has crossed the threshold of the bedroom and is now walking on carpet. A few moments later there is a bump on the side of the bed. I feel hot breath in my face. I hear a plaintive piping sound – meep, meep. I reach out and stroke a furry head. Damp whiskers butt against my hand. I stretch out and fumble for the alarm clock, a small electric one I bought for £2.75 when I first moved to London nearly thirty years ago. At some point the lid of the battery section has been lost and now, when I lift it and try to find the button that makes the face light up, the battery falls out. I rummage on the bedside table for it, almost upsetting a glass of water. A book tumbles to the floor. I find the battery, slot it back into the clock and push the button. I stare at the hands on the clock. They are blurred. For a brief moment I think that we have all overslept and my eleven-year-old daughter has missed the school bus. Then the hands come into better focus and I realise that it is not twenty-five past eight but twenty to five. 'Too early, Manny,' I hiss.

I put the clock back. I shove the dog away, 'It's pitch dark. Go back to your bed.' There is silence. Then the sound of footsteps on the wooden floor, the squeak of a floorboard and the rummaging sound of Little Man (to give him his full name) circling round on his beanbag in front of the stove in the sitting room. I close my eyes.

Squeak, patter, patter, silence, bump, meep, meep. I reach for the clock. Press the button. It still says twenty to five. The battery must have fallen out of it when I put it down. I find my watch. I stare hopefully at it in the black-ness, but the watch is even older than the alarm clock, purchased in the Persian Gulf when I was seventeen, and all its luminosity wore off long ago. I stretch for the light switch. The angle-poise flashes on like an explosion. I squint at the watch, at Manny. 'It's only fifteen minutes since you were last here,' I say. 'Look,' I wave a hand towards the curtains. 'Look. Outside. No. Sun. Nothing. Dark. Black. Go back to bed.' I turn off the light. Patter, patter, squeak, scrunch, scrunch. I close my eyes. I remem-ber the battery and put it back in the clock. I close my eyes again.

Squeak, patter, patter, silence, bump, meep, meep. I pat Manny's head. I reach for the clock. Five thirty-five. A vague grey light is faintly discernible through the curtains. 'Still too early,' I say.

'Meep, meep,' Manny replies.

'No,' I say. 'No way. It's still dark.'

Manny leans his head to one side and starts sliding it back and forth along the duvet, banging his nose against my arm. 'Oh, hell,' I say after a minute of this gentle buf-feting. 'What's the point? I'd never get to sleep anyway.'

I get out of bed. My clothes are on a chair. The T-shirt is inside the shirt, which is in turn inside a zipped-up fleece. I pick them up and force them over my head. Members of Special Forces can dismantle and reassemble a machine gun blindfolded; I can put on five layers of clothing in total darkness without waking the rest of the family.

I step around the bed, feeling ahead for the doorway. I bump into a wardrobe. Kick a shoe. Finally feel the doorframe. Out in the corridor, light the shade of raw pastry is filtering through from the kitchen windows. In a corner of the sitting room the red display on the DVD player glows. I gaze across at it. The whole room seems encased in a shifting fog. It is so early in the morning it's as if the pixels that form the world have not yet got around to coalescing. I blink at the DVD display. 5:48.

I pull on my already laced boots, haul on my anorak, pick up the retractable lead. I look around. Manny is sitting in the corridor. I shake the leader. He watches me unmoved. 'Well, come on,' I hiss. 'You wanted this, not me.' I crouch down and he trots across. We walk out through the front door into a world the colour of a tramp's vest. The sun has not yet raised itself sufficiently to bring colour to the world. Everything is murky monochrome. 'This is the last time,' I say to Manny as I unlatch the front gate. 'You understand? The last time.' He looks up expectantly and wags his tail, his expression is gleeful, 'Come on, then,' I say. 'Let's go.'

January

My dog Manny is a petit basset griffon Vendéen. The name is almost as long as he is, but not quite. Basset griffons are scent hounds. When I told a friend of mine from London that he said, 'What, you mean he hunts perfume?' He had a vision of a shaggy dog chasing through Penhaligon's on the trail of an eau de toilette with citric overtones and a delicate hint of sandalwood. Which is not the case, of course, though sometimes I think it would make life easier if it were.

In the house, Manny can hardly bear to be parted from human company. If you go in the bathroom you can be certain that he'll be sitting dutifully by the door when you come out. In the open air, though, he's a completely different creature. Unclip his leader and he sticks his nose up, nostrils twitching, and hurtles off into the distance without once looking back. Scent hounds have been bred to be independent. Most dogs follow you, scent hounds expect you to follow them.

Our previous dog Ingemar the standard schnauzer was a much bigger and more macho dog than Manny. He wouldn't let other dogs across the threshold of our house and he fought, or attempted to fight, with every male he met, including, on one frankly rather Jerry Springer-like occasion, his own father. Despite his high level of masculine feistiness Ingo hated to take the lead. This would have been fine, except for one thing: he only ever realised this once he was out in front. Walking along a narrow path with him consisted of a round of stops and starts. He'd be loitering behind, then he'd be gripped with the idea of command and barge his way to the front. Once he got there it would suddenly dawn on him that he was in the lead and he'd panic and stop dead in his tracks, and whoever had previously been at the front until Ingo overtook them, would trip over him and curse. Over the course of a mile this might happen a dozen times. Ingo liked the thrill of leadership, but he couldn't take the responsibility. Somewhere in his mind was the knowledge that he wasn't actually the leader, that if he set off in one direction those behind might just head off in another and when he looked around he would find himself alone.

Manny has no such fear. I once read that you could always tell somebody who went to a grand public school because if you met him in the street you ended up walking in the same direction he was going, even if you actually wanted to go the opposite way entirely. Manny didn't go to a grand public school, but he has the confidence of his breeding.

The basset griffon is a hunting dog. The original French hunting hound was something like the shaggy-coated griffon Nivernais, a dog that can trace its antecedents back to the painted caves of Lascaux. The griffon Nivernais, like its cousins the grand griffon Vendéen and grand fauve de Bretagne is a large breed used for *la grande vénerie* – deer and wild boar. In France only the aristocracy were allowed to hunt on horseback and you needed to be mounted to follow a griffon. So the peasants bred a type of griffon they could follow on foot: a sawn-off version. Basset comes from the French for 'low'. On his short legs, the basset griffon would trot along at a pace a pedestrian could just about keep up with and, in case they couldn't, it was also bred to signal its whereabouts by baying and yelping. When Little Man is on a trail the noises he makes are high-pitched and excited, like the distant sound of an infant school playground at break time. Huntsmen call this sound the hound's 'note'. The note of the basset griffon is so loud and so cunningly pitched that you can hear it from a long, long way off. When we were on holiday on the Isle of Mull one Easter I climbed to the top of Beinn Chreagach. Beinn Chreagach is 1200 feet high. As I sat on the summit eating some sandwiches I heard an unmistakable piping bark. I took out a pair of binoculars and, sure enough, there were my partner Catherine and daughter Maisie walking Manny on a beach a couple of miles away.

There are two types of basset griffon Vendéen, the petit and the grand (there is also a medium sized dog, the briquet griffon Vendéen, which is the size of a springer spaniel). The grand is slightly taller at the shoulder and reputedly less mercurial than the little version. All these breeds came originally from a *département* of France on the Atlantic coast south of Brittany. If anybody in Britain has heard of the Vendée it is usually because there's a round-the-world yacht race named in its honour. The other export from the Vendée that you sometimes come across in Britain is a breed of sheep, the Vendéen. The Vendéen's most notable characteristics are ruddy cheeks and bushy whiskers that give it the appearance of a Dickensian coachman.

To the French, the Vendée is a byword for backwardness. During the 1998 World Cup I shared a compartment on the long train journey from Bordeaux to Lyon with an old lady from Verdun and a young man from Cholet, which was not only in the Vendée but – even more excitingly – also had a Womble named after it. The young man from Cholet was neatly dressed and immaculately coiffed and manicured. He worked on a cruise liner as a cabin steward. 'Ooh,' the old woman said cheerily, 'maybe you'll get to meet a rich American lady and marry her.' The young man from Cholet smiled seraphically at the old lady and cocked an eyebrow in my direction because, to be honest, he couldn't have been more obviously gay than if he'd worn a Judy Garland Appreciation Society T-shirt and a leather cap. 'The Vendée is nice,' he said. 'Very pretty. But it is very conservative, very behind everywhere else. You know what the other French say about us? They say that if the end of the world is coming, move to the Vendée. It won't reach there for another twenty years at least.'

The basset griffon shares some of the physical characteristics of the basset hound. It has the same long ears, bowed back-legs and deep chest. In temperament, though, it is quite different. The people of the Vendée are renowned for being stubborn and independent and it is said that the dogs they bred inherited these characteristics. 'They have great charm and a certain charisma,' the huntsman George Johnston wrote of the basset griffons in his book *The Hounds of France*. 'There is nothing sad or reposeful about them, on the contrary they are active and have a distinctive head carriage, it is held high, challenging all comers in a "What I have I hold" attitude.' That seemed to me a perfect summary.

Aside from backwardness, cussedness and a famous and bloody revolt against the French Republic in 1793 that left the region devastated, the Vendée is also well known in France for its expanse of wild country, the *bocage vendéen*, a great wooded thicket of gorse and hawthorn. This *bocage* was the country the basset griffon Vendéen were bred to hunt in. That's why they have a shaggy, coarse coat and an apparent total indifference towards things getting stuck to them. Most dogs will pick incessantly at burrs and twigs that get entangled in their fur, but Little Man is impervious to such concerns. Quite often he curls up in bed with burdocks and lengths of bramble bush all over him. Left to his own devices he would look like a garden bonfire.

In the Vendée and across France they hunted with packs of basset griffons. It was the most popular hunting dog in the country and rarely kept as a pet. When we stayed at a rented apartment in Paris the lady who owned it invited us to her apartment for a drink. The Parisian lady had one of those little Parisian dogs – part Chihuahua, part gerbil. The dog had sandy fur and pointy ears and the lady called it Isis because she thought it looked Egyptian. She asked us if we had a dog. We told her we did and that he was a petit basset griffon Vendéen. The lady nodded, 'Ah,' she said approvingly. '*C'est un chien sportif.*' I liked the idea of a *chien sportif.*

Quite what the basset griffon Vendéen were used to hunt remained sketchy to me. Some Anglophone breed books say rabbits and hares, others, that they are for driving game birds, others claim small deer, or even boar. When it came to foreign working breeds this haziness was fairly common. A similar thing occurs with standard schnauzers. Some say they were carriage dogs, others that they travelled on carts with the itinerant peddlers of

Baden-Wurtemburg. It seemed to me to depend on the world view of the writer. Some like a dog that is doughty, tough and working-class, others want something noble and gallant. Personally, I tend towards the former point of view: not for any political reasons but because I think it is hard to be noble and gallant when you spend a percentage of every day licking your own privates.

What was certain was that these *chiens sportifs* were not generally expected to kill their prey. Their job was to lead the huntsman to it so he could finish it off with a gun. One afternoon, Manny chased a rabbit that had got into the garden and managed to get it trapped in a corner between a fence and the dry stone wall. Once it was there, he sat down and watched it. And when I ran over he looked up at me with what I can only describe as a happy and expectant expression. 'I've done my bit,' he seemed to be saying. 'Now it's your turn.' Not being *un homme sportif*, I let the rabbit go. That night it bit the heads off an entire row of marigolds. Sometimes mercy is overrated.

The petit basset griffon Vendéen gradually spread across France until there were believed to be several hundred thousand of them in working packs. The splendidly named Sir Rupert Buchanan-Jardine of Milk Castle brought the first imports to Britain in the 1930s, but the War soon curtailed any attempt to popularise them and the current generation didn't actually get here until 1969. In some ways, the swinging sixties were probably as good a time as any for a shaggy-haired dog to turn up on these shores. When I mentioned Manny to my cousin, a keen shooting man with a pair of working spaniels, he said, 'Oh yes, I know those. They look very "Wow, like, heavy, man."'

I said that Manny's coat is coarse and shaggy and that's

true of most of it, the white part. But Manny also has tan and brown patches (he is what the breed books call a tricolore) and these are smooth, like the coat of a Labrador. The upshot of all this clever breeding is that Manny has a large head, short bowed legs, long pendulous ears, a vigorously wagging tail and a long shaggy coat, except where it is short and smooth. He looks, as one friend put it, like several other dogs squashed together. This rather ad hoc appearance puzzles quite a lot of people who meet him. 'Isn't he lovely,' they say. 'Do you know what his parents were?' Manny looks like a mutt, but he can trace his ancestors back to the sixteenth century. He is an aristocrat in mufti.

Experts believe that a scent hound's sense of smell may be a million times more sensitive than that of a human. That is quite an extraordinary thing. If a man or woman had a similar ability they'd be slapped on the pages of Marvel or DC comics right next to Spiderman and the Human Torch.

Scent is left on the ground by tread, but it also floats in the air. Particles lift from the ground due to evaporation, or hang there after an animal has passed by. It isn't only fear of being seen that lead many creatures to stay motionless when they are under threat. Just as the human eye detects movement faster than it does shapes or colours, so the hound's nose detects a moving animal quicker than one that is standing still.

Everything about Manny's head is designed to help him smell. His long whiskers dust the ground and when he bends over something his ears fall forwards so that they form a cowl, trapping in the scent like the hoods worn by obsessive French gastronomes when tucking into a meal of fresh truffles. Like all scent hounds Manny produces a lot of drool when he is sniffing something. He smells not just through his nose but through his tongue as well. When his beard is thoroughly sodden he'll shake his head and slather will fly in every direction. Sometimes going for a walk with him is like being at a punk rock concert in 1977.

Once he has a scent it's more or less impossible to predict in which direction he'll go. His vision of the world is based on what he can smell rather than what he can see. Scent is so powerful to him that when he encounters something particularly pungent and fresh he leaps back from it as if it has slapped him round the snout. Sometimes it seems to produce almost a narcotic effect, sending Manny into another world where it is almost impossible to reach him.

When we both stand at the edge of a field the information our brains process about it are totally different. To me it is grass, forget-me-nots, patches of wild violets, a row of ash trees, a post-and-rail fence. To Manny it is an intricately woven tapestry of odours that tell him not just what is here now, but what has been here in the hours before we arrived. The recent past looms larger in his vision of the world than it does in mine. Where a rabbit is at this moment ('Look, it's over there, Manny!') appears less important to him than where it was an hour ago ('This is where it was at sunrise, Harry!'). A scent hound is an historian. He follows the trail of the past knowing that eventually it will lead to the present.

When he is on a trail Manny is unstoppable. He never looks back to see where you are. He is the only dog I have ever owned who will disappear over the horizon. Most working dogs need a constant stream of instructions from a human. Scent hounds don't. They carry their instructions in their genes. 'Find it!' the instructions say and that is what they do. Humans follow them. That's the deal.

The schnauzer hunted too but Ingo, like most dogs, hunted by sight. Dogs that hunt by sight do so silently. The only time Ingo barked when he was chasing something was when his quarry was too big for him to bring down on his own – a deer, perhaps, or a cyclist.

Ingo liked to hunt rabbits. At first he rushed blindly after them the second he saw them. But he wasn't fast enough to catch them that way so, after a while, he changed tactics. He started to approach them slowly, gradually dropping his head and body lower to the ground as he did so. It took me quite a while to figure out what he was up to.

A rabbit's eyes are on either side of its head. This means that a rabbit has fantastic peripheral vision, but is unable to judge distances. A rabbit literally cannot get things into perspective. As a consequence rabbits think that if something is getting bigger it is advancing towards them and if it is getting smaller it is retreating. Ingo had worked that out. He knew he wasn't quick enough to rush a rabbit from a long way off, so he was using his superior intelligence.

Not that it worked, I should add. Because what happened with Ingo was this: he advanced toward the rabbit, getting lower and lower and gradually slower and slower, until he was within ten yards of it, and then he stopped. I could sense that he was willing himself to charge but nothing happened. The part of his brain that should have ordered him to 'Go, go, go' had frozen. He was suffering from the hunting dog's equivalent of the yips. For years the great German golfer Bernhard Langer would find himself drawing his putter back to strike the ball only for his hands and arms to lock. A canine version of the same psychological complaint had affected my dog.

Mr Dodds was the first dog-related acquaintance I had made. I met him the first time I took Ingemar for a walk and from then on, for a decade or so, I bumped into him every morning. Mr Dodds was a retired farmer. He had a strong Northumbrian accent, one of the last of a breed who still talked with the authentic rolling, phlegmy 'r' that was said to have been affected originally in homage to the speech impediment of Harry Hotspur, the fifteenth-century Duke of Northumberland. Maybe that was right but to most outsiders it conjured up images of Edith Piaf. And besides, when you came across somebody as tough, violent and heavily armed as Harry Hotspur I'd imagine the last thing you'd want to do is imitate his speech impediment: 'Art thou taking the pith?' Crunch!

A small man who stooped perpetually forward as if walking into a stiff wind, Mr Dodds had a wrinkled and weather-beaten face that put me in mind of an overripe orange pippin. That, at least, was how he looked when he was out walking the dog. One day when I was in the bank a smart elderly fellow in a tweed jacket tapped me on the shoulder. 'Now then, young man,' the smart man said. 'What are you up to?' I had no idea who he was at first, but as I chatted with him it gradually dawned on me that it was Mr Dodds. He'd been to a lunch at the cattle mart. It was the first time I'd ever seen him with his dentures in. It's amazing what a difference a set of teeth make to a face.

Mr Dodds' dog was a corgi named Taffy. Most people in Britain nowadays associate corgis with the Queen and judge it a bit of a lapdog. Mr Dodds had used Taffy for the corgi's real purpose, as a herding dog on his farm. Taffy was black and tan. His foxy face had a no-nonsense set to it. 'I've had that little beggar for thret-teen years,' Mr Dodds said, 'and you know what? If I turn my back on him for two minute he still runs up and bites me.'

'Really,' I said.

'Oh aye,' Mr Dodds said. 'He likes to keep me on my toes.'

It sounded to me as if Mr Dodds and Taffy were like Inspector Clouseau and his manservant Cato in the Pink Panther films. I imagined Taffy leaping from behind doorways and darting out from under beds when Mr Dodds least expected it. I saw Mr Dodds, involved in filling out some complex form about EU milk yield quotas, yelling 'Not now, Taffy!' as the corgi dived on him from the top of a light fitting.

Later I suffered similar problems with Ingemar. It wasn't that he attacked me if my back was turned (or that he jumped from light fittings), it was just that if I played with him he would start off quite gently, but slowly he'd start to bite. And the bites would gradually get harder and harder. Ingo had a particular ability to locate joints and knuckles, and when he darted in and grabbed your ankle or wrist it hurt. Eventually he'd push too far and I'd end up having to grab hold of him and wrestle him to the ground until he did the dog submission thing of going limp.

'Why does he do that?' Catherine asked one day after Ingo and I had had a prolonged tussle on the front lawn.

'I think he's testing me,' I said. 'He wants to be the alpha male in the pack. He knows I'm older than he is and he's checking to see if I'm weakening. One day he reckons

I'll be too old and decrepit to fight him off and when that happens he'll take charge.'

'And you'll be forced to limp around outside, living off scraps and curling up in the coal shed,' Catherine said with a chuckle.

'You're laughing now,' I said, 'but remember: if he does triumph it won't be me he's expecting to sleep with.'

One evening Manny suddenly jumped up from the mat in front of the stove, trotted over to the daybed we have under the front window, jumped on it and stared out into the darkness, cocking his head from one side to the other, listening to some sound that baffled him. Catherine got up and went over to him. She listened too. 'Oh, God,' she said. 'They're at it again. You'd think they could find somewhere else.'

I knew exactly who 'they' were and what they were doing. We had first noticed it the second January after we had moved to Northumberland. It was around midnight and Catherine and I had just finished watching a very scary French film called *La Cérémonie* in which Isabelle Hupert plays a homicidal postmistress and Sandrine Bonnaire, her accomplice, sports a haircut so appalling even Elton John's wigmaker would have rejected it. Our nerves were already jangling when, from outside, we heard a terrible screeching noise. It was the sound of an animal in agony. We went out into the garden with a torch. Ingemar came with us, but as soon as he heard the awful yowling he began to bark and bounce angrily up and down, all his legs stiff and straight, so he looked like he was mounted on four pogo-sticks. I took him indoors and told him to wait quietly. I knew that the minute I went out he'd issue his protest at such shoddy treatment by jumping on all the chairs he was forbidden to go on when we were around. He had a peculiar morality about the chairs, Ingemar. He didn't go on them if you were in another part of the house. Even if you were locked in the bathroom he stayed down. But the minute you stepped out of the front door and closed it – bang, he was straight on the sofa: 'I am the master now.' Once Catherine had gone outside to collect something from our neighbours Ossie and Nora. They turned out to be sitting in deckchairs in their back garden, which had a direct view in through our bedroom window. 'When I got round there I could see Ingo bouncing up and down on the bed,' Catherine said. 'I bet when we're out for the evening he plays loud music and smokes.'

The horrific keening was coming from somewhere in the wood at the bottom of the garden. The local landowner had been using the disused quarry that formed one edge of it as a refuse dump. 'It sounds like something's trapped,' I said.

'It'll be caught up in all that wire and junk,' Catherine replied.

Recalling scenes from various big game hunting movies I'd watched as a boy I counselled against going into the trees to take a look, 'An animal is at its most dangerous when wounded or cornered, or both,' I said, in a voice that I hoped conveyed a deep knowledge of bush lore rather than simple cowardice. 'We should phone the RSPCA. They'll know what to do.'

So we went indoors, found the number in the phone-book and Catherine rang them. She explained the situation. 'Well, it's an awful noise,' I heard her say. 'I don't know, sort of a yowling scream I suppose. It's been going on for ages. Yes, I can still hear it. I can take the phone outside and then you can hear it too, if that's a help? OK, I'll do that.' Catherine took the phone and we both went outside. The grisly yelping was if anything even noisier than before. Catherine held the phone up in the direction of the sound.

'Did you hear that?' she asked the RSPCA man. 'Yes, that was the noise. I thought it was a fox! Oh . . . Oh, right. Are you sure? It sounded in awful pain. Ah. Mmm. I see. How embarrassing. Well, it's kind of you to say so. I'm really sorry to have bothered you. Thanks. Bye.'

Catherine and I went back indoors with the phone. 'It's a female fox,' Catherine said. 'And a male fox. Having sex. The RSPCA man was very nice about it. He said he gets at least a dozen phone calls every December and January.'

'It was very loud,' I said. 'In fact, it was the noisiest sex I've ever heard. It was several decibels higher than those two German students who lived in the flat downstairs from us in Clapham, and when they got going windows used to rattle and pictures fell off the wall. It was like when the admiral fires his cannon in *Mary Poppins*.'

'Yes,' Catherine said, 'but I suppose at least the foxes don't play "Zoom" by Fat Larry's Band as part of the mating ritual.'

February

It was after we had been living in Northumberland for a year that we decided to get a dog. I knew what dog I wanted. I had known it for thirty years, since an afternoon in a bar in Cologne where the bar-owner's dog kept wandering over to the table I was sitting at with a friend of mine, gently untying our shoe laces and then sauntering off again. The dog had a chunky body, salt-and-pepper coloured coat, a bushy beard and moustaches and severe eyebrows. It looked at once stern and comical, like a cartoon of a strict professor. When I got home I looked in a dog book in the village library and found out what it was: a standard schnauzer.

So Catherine and I set out to find a standard schnauzer. This proved to be more difficult than we'd thought. You see quite a few miniature schnauzers around Britain but standards are altogether less common. In the days before the Internet the only way we had of finding dogs for sale was looking in the classified ads in the local and regional papers. We telephoned the Standard Schnauzer Society and a lady there said she thought there might be a litter due somewhere in Westmoreland sometime, but she wasn't sure and could we call again? But when we did there was just an answer machine and nobody phoned back.

One day our local paper had an advert in the pets' section for some spinone pups. I had seen a spinone at a game fair in Teesdale. Like the schnauzer they had a fine beard and their general appearance reminded me of the Colonel in Walt Disney's *101 Dalmatians*. We had been searching fruitlessly for a schnauzer for several months; maybe it was time to give up. I could get a spinone and call him Primo after Primo Carnera, the Italian World Heavyweight Champion boxer of the 1930s who had been so huge and so slow the US press had nicknamed him 'The Amblin' Alp'. I could picture Primo lolloping around our garden. I wrote down the number. I would call them in the morning.

That night I turned out the light and lay in the dark. A picture popped into my mind and would not go away. It was of a standard schnauzer sitting in a vast and empty field. His head was held high and cocked slightly to one side as if he was listening for something: as if he was listening for someone to call him. And I knew that if I bought a spinone that schnauzer would sit faithfully waiting forever for a call that would never come. So I got up, found the telephone number I had written down and threw it on the fire. Then I blew my nose and went back to bed.

A few days later my father called. He'd been talking to a woman at work who bred dachshunds, he said, and she knew a man who bred giant schnauzers and she'd asked him about standards and he'd told her there was a breeder near Longtown who had pups due in April. 'If you've got a pen handy I'll give you the details,' Dad said. And that was how we got Ingemar.

So I know where the idea to get a standard schnauzer came from, but I'm not quite so sure how we settled on a petit basset griffon Vendéen. I seem to recall trawling through endless dog websites looking at photos and thinking, Yes, that one looks good, in much the same way I had, as a child, spent endless hours staring at a matchbox cars catalogue trying to determine how to spend next week's pocket money.

What settled it though was when we took things to the next stage and started looking at breed sites. We found one devoted to petit basset griffon Vendéen that included a video clip of a PBGV (as we now knew to call them) hunting along a lakeside track and a sound file that allowed you to listen to a female basset griffon baying. The sound of that yodelling call was enough to convince us.

I should say that this was a US website. I was glad we had found it first. The UK websites that carried information about basset griffons were altogether more discouraging. 'Not a dog for anyone in a hurry,' one declared. 'If you cannot spare two hours to go searching for your dog when they disappear after a game on a weekday morning, then you shouldn't even consider this breed.' Another advised that the PBGV 'is a very vocal dog and noise may be a nuisance' and admonished the prospective buyer to 'be warned: this breed can escape from even the most apparently secure garden and once gone it will be your responsibility to find him.'

The US websites by contrast were full of uplifting snippets: 'Not for nothing are they called the happy breed,' they chirruped. 'This smiling little fellow will bring untold joy into your lives.' Behaviour that was a major headache to British breeders was the sort of mischievous rascality that warmed American hearts.

'Can I keep this dog in a city apartment?' one questioner from Wisconsin asked.

'You bet!' came the perky reply. 'As long as you have a park nearby or can drive out to the country as part of your daily routine your basset griffon will love his urban home.'

I suspected that if a British website had been asked the same question they'd have advised the questioner to save the money he was going to spend on the dog and use it instead to pay for a psychiatrist, or better yet, buy a rope and a chair to jump off.

This gap between British and US attitudes was not a surprise to me because I had, over the years, read a number of writing guides from both sides of the Atlantic. If you looked at a UK writers' guide it was full of negatives. After reading it any would-be writer would have gone away with the impression that even to think of getting work published was as laughably naïve as sending your credit card details to somebody in Nigeria in return for a share of the vast fortune in gold and diamonds that was currently locked in a Swiss vault following the sad and unexpected death of Dr Wednesday Akruna. The American guides by contrast were hugely uplifting. You are talented, they said. You are driven! You are great! If you read the US writers' guides you went away with the idea that all you had to do was type the name on the top of a sheet of A4 and some publisher somewhere on the planet would pay you $500 for it.

It was through a website that we found Little Man. He was a year old and located with his breeder not far up the A1. It was early February and we set off in a blizzard. The Automobile Association was advising travellers to stay at home unless their journey was really necessary. Our journey was really necessary because experience with dog breeders suggested that if you showed even the slightest sign of weakness they'd dismiss you like a shot. A friend of ours had tried to buy a Norfolk Terrier. She'd found a breeder down south who had a litter due. When the litter was born the breeder phoned our friend. She and her family were away for the weekend. The breeder left two messages. The second one was rather curt, 'If you are the sort of person who goes away when they know their puppy is about to be born, then I don't think you are the sort of person I want to have one of my dogs,' he said. 'Goodbye.'

Our friend phoned him up when she got back, but he was adamant that her cavalier attitude disqualified her from dog ownership. 'Apparently I was supposed to wait by the phone,' our friend said later, 'pacing up and down the corridor anxiously smoking a cigar and waiting for news from the midwife.'

The PBGV breeder's house, like many dog breeders' homes, was a monument to her chosen dog. There were petit basset griffon Vendéen drinks coasters, scatter cushions, mugs, tea trays, découpage pictures and embroidered samplers. The wall clock above the table had the face of a PBGV printed on it; so did the doormat. There were basset griffon fridge magnets stuck to every metal surface, like barnacles on a wrecked hull.

'I'll call them in,' the breeder said. She opened the kitchen door onto a plain corridor that ran out to a rear kennel block and whistled. A few seconds later a swirling mass of dogs burst into the room. They circled it at high speed, while the breeder yelled 'That's Molly, that's Polly, that's Sally, that's Solly, and that one there on the left . . . on the right . . . in the middle, is the pup.' When they had

done three laps they rushed out again and the breeder
shut the door. 'So, what do you think of him, then?' she
asked.

'He looks like quite a fellow,' I said.

'He's amazing,' Maisie said.

'He's lovely,' Catherine said.

We discussed the breed, what they ate, how much exercise and grooming they needed. The breeder grilled us on
our previous dog-handling experience. Getting a pedigree
dog is a lot harder than getting a child. When you have a
baby the nurse comes out from the maternity ward to
check you have a proper car seat and then away you go.
Nobody asks you if you have an enclosed garden, previous
childcare experience, or questions you closely to see
whether you really know what you are letting yourself in
for, or are just one of those dumb idiots who's seen a baby
bundling about in a TV ad and thought they looked really,
really, like, cute. You had to be well prepared and on your
toes with dog breeders.

'The petit basset griffon is a big character,' the PBGV
breeder said.

I was ready for this. 'We had a standard schnauzer,' I
said.

'Dog or bitch?'

'A dog,' I said. The breeder looked at me with what I
imagined to be a degree of newfound respect, because
while standard schnauzer bitches are considered very bid-
dable, the male standard schnauzer has a reputation for
being 'a big character'. In the world of pedigree dogs the
phrase 'a big character' is usually a euphemism for 'hard
to control'. (In the world of humans it generally means
something similar, with added alcohol.)

'What happened to him?' the breeder asked.

'He died last year.'

'What did he die of?'

'A lung infection.'

'How old was he?'

'Thirteen.'

'Are you house-proud?' the breeder suddenly asked Catherine sternly. 'Because if you like a clean house you don't want one of these. They are,' the breeder said, 'a magnet for muck.'

This was true enough as we soon discovered. The PBGV's low-slung body and long rough coat attracted dirt better than a vacuum cleaner. Manny could have picked up mud walking across the lobby of the Ritz.

We assured her that we were not really house-proud (while pointing out that there was obviously no danger of the dog getting sick due to lack of hygiene either). We told her that we were country people, had a big garden (largely unkempt – dig away in the flower beds, little fellow, you'll hear no complaints from us!) and that there was someone in the house practically twenty-four hours a day and sometimes even longer than that. 'You're very welcome to come up and look,' we said. The breeder said she might well do that.

'Do you want another look at him before you go?' the breeder asked. We said we would love one. She opened the kitchen door and whistled. The pack came hurtling in again, a big rolling mass of fur and flapping ears. 'That's the pup,' the breeder said, pointing as they sped round the room and then out again.

As we drove away in the swirling snow I said, 'Well, he was great, wasn't he?'

'Really fantastic,' Catherine said.

'Which one was he exactly?' Maisie said.

I looked at Catherine. She shook her head. 'Well,' I said, 'we're not actually certain but I thought they were all really nice, didn't you?'

It was raining. I always had trouble getting Little Man to go out in the rain. He doesn't like it. He doesn't like the sound it makes when cars drive through it, he doesn't like the fact it washes away the scent trails he loves to follow. But most of all he doesn't like getting his feet wet. Manny skips around puddles and jumps over streams. I have never known a dog with such an aversion to water. The trouble with most dogs is keeping them out of water, not getting them into it. Ingemar the schnauzer could have located a muddy puddle in the Sahara Desert. And once he'd found it, he'd have walked the length of it, stomped back again just to make sure, and then jumped on the first Tuareg he saw wearing white trousers.

Manny, though, has only been in water voluntarily once in his life. That was when he chased a moorhen and her chicks across the string of small, reedy islands that ran out into the river like a chilly miniature version of the Florida Keys. He'd been so excited about the hunt he hadn't noticed he was sploshing through up to his hocks. But when he got to the final island and the moorhen set sail across to the opposite bank, her fluffy infants straining to keep pace at her tail, and he realised what he had done, he panicked. He ran round and round desperately looking for a way off the island that didn't involve crossing the river, but he couldn't find one. Every once in a while he'd stop and tentatively wave a paw over the water, but he couldn't bring himself to take the plunge. Eventually he stopped running, found a spot where he could look directly at me and started barking. 'Oh no,' I bellowed back, 'absolutely not. If you think I'm wading out there and carrying you back, you can think again.'

Manny looked at me and barked some more.

'Do I look as if I'm mental?' I said. 'You're a dog. I've got new trainers on. It's only water. Come on here and don't be so stupid.'

Manny barked again.

'No way. No chance. You can sit there all day. See if I care,' I yelled.

Manny began to howl pitifully.

Five minutes later I was wading knee deep through the shallows with a shivering wet dog on my shoulder.

And that was the last time we did that. Now if he comes to a stretch he can't go over or round he turns back, even if it's half an inch deep. If I try to lead him across it he struggles out of his collar and runs round in a circle, belly low to the ground, barking and wagging his tale. He's scared that I'll be angry with him, but he's even more scared of getting wet.

Today I had to pick Manny up and carry him over the large puddle that had formed outside the gate and out into the lane. Otherwise we wouldn't have a walk at all. It made me think about something else Manny does. Every time we open the door into the porch he runs in, picks up a shoe and runs off with it. You can hear his nails tick-tocking across the wood floor in the passageway and then there's a clunk as he drops it. Thirty seconds later he comes scampering back in and grabs another. And so it goes on. He doesn't chew the shoes. He doesn't shake them, or toss them about. He just carries them away and leaves them in a pile by the sitting room door.

Once, when I was out walking Ingo many years ago, I met a man with a brown and white terrier. The man's name was Tommy but everyone in the village called him 'Tucker' after the nursery rhyme Northumbrian children sing to the tune of 'Frère Jacques'. Tucker was in his late sixties. He spent his time walking the dog, growing leeks and moaning about Newcastle United. 'You need to keep busy,' he said.

Tucker was watching for a stoat that had disappeared into a tangled patch of long grass and lady's smock. 'You see this,' he said and he made a squeaky, chirruping noise. Straight away the stoat's ginger head popped up above the grass and began twisting round like a periscope. 'Can't resist it,' the man chuckled. 'Even though there's two people and two dogs here and he knows he should be hiding. They hear anything that sounds like food and they're up.'

Unlike Kenneth Grahame, who viewed all members of the family Mustilidae as vermin of the lowest stamp, Tommy admired stoats. He said they kept the rat population down. He thought they were fearless and doughty. They have to be, he said. When a stoat killed a rabbit it was outweighed by about 500 per cent. 'It's like me or you fighting a camel,' he said.

Tucker had once been a miner. He'd spent his working life underground, hacking fluorspar from crooked seams in the North Pennines so that someone else could turn it into paint. Tommy Tucker's dog was called Tadger.

Tadger was a rescue dog. Tommy had got him from the RSPCA pound. He said that when he went in all the other dogs ran down to the front barking and wagging their tails, but Tadger had just stood on his own in one corner doing back flips. 'I thought that's the lad for me,' Tommy said. I could imagine Tadger doing back flips, because he was an acrobatic little fellow. When he came to greet you he'd run forward and suddenly execute a series of forward rolls until he was right at your feet at which point he bounced upright wagging his tail. If he'd been human he'd have yelled 'Ta-rah!'

Now Tadger was digging out stones, picking them up in his mouth and carrying them to a spot next to an old alder stump. After a while he had erected a small, neat pile. 'Does he always do that?' I asked.

'Oh aye,' Tucker said. 'If ever I stop still while I'm out he starts up with it. He's had them three feet high before now.' I asked him if he had any idea why the dog did it. 'I suppose he's marking his territory,' he said. 'Other dogs cock their legs. He builds a monument.'

I looked at the mound of stones and a thought occurred to me. 'I suppose,' I said, 'he must be a cairn terrier, then?' Tommy looked at me as if I was a total idiot, 'Nah, he's a Jack Russell cross,' he said.

For a while I'd thought Manny was doing the same as Tucker's dog only with shoes instead of pebbles. Today as I watched him dodging the rivulets of rainwater that were scuttering and bubbling down the lane I started to wonder. Maybe he was carrying the shoes off for a different purpose – so he could try them on. Perhaps he was desperately searching for a couple of pairs that fitted so that he'd never have to get his paws soaked again.

It was in February that I first met Mrs Pelham-Beale. She came striding towards me through a miniature honour guard of snowdrops and aconites. Mrs Pelham-Beale was very tall and big boned and had a drawn, aristocratic face with cheeks so sunken that when I first met her I assumed she was sucking on a particularly toothsome boiled sweet. If there had ever been a version of *Stars in Their Eyes* for posh people she would have been a brilliant Eleanor Roosevelt.

Mrs Pelham-Beale had a very powerful voice. Whether this was due to deafness or simply because she was used to shouting at the lower orders I never discovered. The volume was hardly an aid to communication because Mrs Pelham-Beale spoke with such an upper class drawl you really had to focus very hard to make out what she was saying. Once I had been in the newsagents when Mrs Pelham-Beale had come in and enquired as to the where-abouts of her favourite magazine and for a moment I had thought there must be a periodical called *Whores and Hinds*.

The difficulty of understanding Mrs Pelham-Beale was increased by her habit, shared by many country landown-ers, of omitting any word she considered just too insultingly little to be bothered with. When the great Regency dandy Beau Brummel was asked if he had ever tried vegetables he replied, 'I think I may once have eaten a pea.' Mrs Pelham-Beale took a similarly haughty line with prepositions and the more diminutive type of verb.

I met Mrs Pelham-Beale when she was out walking her dog, an elderly pug called Benbow. Benbow was named after the eighteenth-century British admiral John Benbow who'd been killed fighting the French in the Caribbean. According to an old sea shanty: 'Brave Benbow lost his legs and so on his stumps he begged, "Fight on, the English lads, to the last, to the last."' Like the great seaman, the pug appeared to be on his last legs too. He had a barrel-shaped body, bowed pins and suffered so badly from emphysema that when he walked he sounded like a punctured harmonium. Mr Dodds told me later that Benbow was the last of a small pack of pugs Mrs Pelham-Beale had once owned, and which had trailed behind her puffing and wheezing when she rode through the village on her horse. 'I always thought,' he said, 'that some day one of them would get crushed under a pile of falling dung.'

Originally imported from China, pugs had once been the dogs of choice for the upper class. In 1572 the King of Holland was saved from an assassin by one of his own pugs. Pugs attended the coronation of William Prince of Orange in 1688 and slept on the matrimonial bed of Napoleon and Josephine. Queen Charlotte, wife of George III, owned half a dozen and Horace Walpole had kept even more at Strawberry Hill, his Gothic mansion in Surrey. They ate at the dining table with him, off porcelain plates, liveried servants drying their mouths with damask napkins. Latterly, however, the Labrador, a dog so solidly middle class it always struck me as the canine equivalent of the Aga and the Volvo estate, had usurped the pug's position in front of the country house fireplace. I took it as a sign of Mrs Pelham-Beale's grandness that she had refused to follow this bourgeois fad and stuck resolutely with the ancient Chinese breed.

The first time we met, Mrs Pelham-Beale glanced at Ingo and bellowed a single word at me. It sounded like 'Izzernaightsah!' I considered for a moment what the word might mean. Mrs Pelham-Beale stared impatiently at me. It was clear she didn't expect to wait long for an answer. I ran the word round my head one more time, then it struck me that perhaps she was fearful that Ingo might attack little Benbow, that she was asking 'Is he a fighter?'

'Oh no,' I said. 'He's very friendly.'

Mrs Pelham-Beale looked at me for a long while as if trying to determine whether I was foreign, deranged or both. 'Nyoh, nyoh,' she roared eventually. 'Not-ah fate-ah, ah zzern aight-sah.'

Somewhere in my brain, cogs revolved and clicked. Once when we'd first moved to Northumberland I had met an old man in the park who had a strong Northumbrian accent. He had begun complaining to me about the fact that one of the benches had been vandalised. 'These young 'uns today,' he said. 'They're 'ticed by bother. If it were down to us I'd fetch the borch.' I puzzled over what he meant for days, wondering if 'borch' was some slang term for a policeman, or a special local magistrate with draconian powers. Then a week later I woke up at three in the morning, slapped my forehead and said, 'Birch! He wanted to whip them with a birch!'

Luckily this time it didn't take seven days to grasp the meaning. 'Ah!' I exclaimed with the glee of somebody finally grasping the answer to a difficult crossword clue. 'Yes, he's a schnauzer all right.'

'Hyan'sum chep,' Mrs Pelham-Beale said.

It is a truth known to all dog lovers that the minute a stranger praises their pet for its sweetness or nobility it will respond by immediately beginning to noisily and fanatically lick its own bottom. Ingemar didn't do that on this occasion. Instead, having just drunk copiously from a large puddle, he belched with Chaucerian vigour.

'Haugh, haugh!' Mrs Pelham-Beale laughed. 'A gentleman, too, I see!'

I rather warmed to her after that.

Late in the month Little Man and I caught the twice-daily bus from Berwick-on-Tweed to Lindisfarne. It was one of those days when the temperature rarely creeps above freezing point and exposed skin tightens until your face feels like it's shrink-wrapped.

The public lavatories on Holy Island are fitted with floor-to-ceiling turnstiles. In the summer tourist season, when the vast car park on the outskirts of the island's only village is overflowing, the mechanisms revolve so rapidly they could easily be harnessed as an alternative energy source to heat and light the homes of Lindisfarne's 160 full-time residents.

Half a million people flock across the three-mile-long causeway from the mainland each year. St Aidan, the Irishman who might be credited with inadvertently starting the tourist rush, arrived in Northumberland in AD 635. He chose Lindisfarne as the seat of his new bishopric, largely because it reminded him of the Hebridean island of Iona.

Come here in the summer – when St Aidan's winery is besieged by coach parties eager to test the reputed aphrodisiac powers of the local mead and the driveway up to the small castle on Beblow Crag is doing a passable imitation of Oxford Street – and it's hard to grasp what might have led the monk to so whimsical a conclusion; Iona, after all, is the personification of Celtic asceticism, while Holy Island is a place where the public lavatories are entered as if they were a football stadium. Arrive in the early morning in deep winter, however, when the tourists are safely tucked up indoors and there's frost, snow and a tear-jerking wind whipping in off the North Sea and it's easy to see why the rigorously spiritual Aidan might have been reminded of his former home.

Manny and I set out across the island. The biscuit-coloured grass along the water's edge was tinged pewter by the frost, and powdered snow whirled around our feet like a theatrical mist. A skein of Canada geese wheeled above the lough and flocks of speckled dunlins skittered in and out of the sea like paddling children.

On a sandy path between the dunes we met a man with a dainty fox terrier. The fox terrier was very upright and straight backed and he moved with tiny, quick steps. He looked as if he was powered by clockwork. The fox terrier beetled towards Manny on his extendable lead, but the owner clicked him to a halt. 'Come away, Julian,' he called with a tug on the lead.

'Julian!' I said to Manny after the fox terrier and his owner were out of earshot. 'Julian! Fancy that.'

Manny didn't respond. He was busy rattling about in a thicket of dead thistles and, to be honest, names are a bit of a delicate topic with him.

When we went to collect Manny the breeder asked if we had considered a name for the dog. Our thinking was that, since the petit basset griffon Vendéen was a French breed, he should have a French name. We wondered about Gaston, or Auguste, or Theophile. We pondered Marcel, D'Artagnan and Gerard, but we couldn't actually imagine shouting any of them. We had named our schnauzer after a famous heavyweight boxer. I thought of other heavy-weight boxers we could name the new dog after. The only Frenchman I could think of who'd fought for the world title was Georges Carpentier, aka 'The Orchid Man'. The name Georges was a bit dull, though, and besides, Jack Dempsey had flattened him. Then an inspiration came to me: Joe Louis. The Vendée had been famously royalist during the French Revolution. Its citizens had tried to assassinate Napoleon and fought a bloody war of resistance under the white and gold banner of the Bourbons. What better name for a dog from the Vendée than Louis?

'Well,' I said to the breeder, 'we'd wondered about "Louis".'

The breeder looked astonished; her eyes widened and then slid sideways to the window outside which her husband was refilling a bird feeder with peanuts. 'Mmm, yes, I suppose, yes, erm . . .' She coughed and reached for a tissue.

'Has he got a name already?' Catherine asked.

'Yes. I mean, we've been calling him Manny because his pedigree name is Little Man. But the name we gave him is . . . David.' Now it was our turn to look astonished and slide our eyes.

'David?' I said eventually.

'Yes,' the lady said. 'The minute I saw him the name came to me. He just looks like a David, don't you think?'

I hadn't really seen enough of the pup to judge, but I thought it altogether unlikely just the same. David. It was like naming a donkey Christopher, or a hamster Phil. It reminded me that once my friend Andy had said that if he ever got a cat he was going to call it Steve. That was a joke, though.

I suppose I should have expected it really. The naming of dogs is as personal a thing as the naming of children. Breeders though seem to have a particularly cloth ear. Perhaps it's because they put so much imagination into the pedigree name that they have nothing left to give when it comes to an everyday handle. If you watch *Crufts Dog Show* on the telly you come across numerous examples. 'And this is Bassenthwaite Blue Mountain Hussar,' commentator Peter Purves would inform viewers over shots of a magnificent-looking otter hound, 'known to his owners as Colin. And following behind him is Paragon Lancelot Chanson de Roland, but we can call him Alan.'

When we had told the man we bought our standard schnauzer from what we were going to call it he had reacted with similar ill-concealed disbelief. As I say, we had chosen the name Ingemar partly in honour of the handsome Swedish boxer Ingemar Johansen and partly because of the little boy in the Lasse Hellstrom film *My Life as a Dog*. We'd chosen a Nordic name after we discovered that a lot of the male standard schnauzers that had come to Britain had been imported from Scandinavia. One of them was Ingemar's grandfather. His name was Olav.

After he'd cleared his throat the schnauzer breeder had said, 'Obviously it's up to you, but I'd rather thought that as his pedigree name is Charlemagne you'd call him Charlie,' he said.

'Or Mangy,' I said to Catherine as we walked back to the car.

'We don't have to call him David, do we?' Maisie asked when we left the basset griffon breeder's house.

'No,' Catherine said, 'I don't think we'll ever call him David.'

'Except,' I said, 'when we want to really annoy him.'

Now I looked at Manny burrowing about in the dried thistles of Holy Island. 'Come along,' I said, but he remained oblivious, tail wagging, head invisible. 'Come along now, *Dave*,' I said. 'We haven't got all day. We need to get back for that bus if we want our tea. I bet Julian's already sitting down to his egg and cress sandwiches.'

March

When we contacted the breeder about Ingemar she told us that we were the only people who had put our names down for a dog, all the other buyers wanted bitches. The reason for this was the male schnauzer's reputation as a larger-than-life personality. As it turned out there were seven pups in the litter and only one dog. So everybody was happy.

The first time we saw Ingemar, he was six weeks old. His eyes were still half-closed and every so often he collapsed on the breeder's carpet and lay there on his tubby little tummy with his front legs splayed out in front of him, squinting like a mole. He had an orange tongue and sometimes when he tried to walk forwards he went backwards instead. He hadn't yet got any teeth and, as a consequence, his mother still loved him dearly and watched us keenly whenever we went near him, or any of his sisters.

The next time we saw Ingemar was when we went to collect him. He was eleven weeks old by then, had teeth like a row of little needles and his mother – fed up with him biting her teats – practically shoved him to us with her snout and then shooed us out of the door.

Dog breeders like to offer strict instructions to new

owners. Usually they will give you a photocopied sheet covered with a detailed list of dos and don'ts. Some are fussier than others. Occasionally they are draconian. When some friends of ours bought a Dandie Dinmont terrier pup his instruction sheet ran to five closely typed pages and included admonitions such as: 'Your dog should never be allowed to jump down from a height of more than seventy centimetres', 'Do not let your dog become accustomed to cushions', 'Never let your dog run up stairs, always carry him' and 'Warning!! Dogs can choke on feathers.'

The sheet of instructions that came with Ingemar was altogether shorter and more sensible. I determined to obey them. Item number seven on the list was strict, but fair. 'Puppy must get used to being on his own. Do not let puppy sleep in your bedroom.' 'Do not' was underlined three times.

We draped a blanket over the kitchen table to make a sort of cave and put Ingo's box under it. We put a hot-water bottle under his blanket to mimic the warmth of his mother and we put a big old-fashioned alarm clock on the table so that the ticking would sound like her heart. We popped Ingo in his new nest, said good night, shut the door and went to bed. We were awoken by the sounds of pitiful whimpering. I went in to see him. Ingemar was standing in the middle of the lino, quivering and bleating with terror. I picked him up and put him back among the blankets. I patted him. I stroked his fur. I assured him that, though everything might seem odd and frightening just at the moment, it was all perfectly safe. Then I went back to bed.

Over the next two nights I got up every hour. On the third night I went to see Ingemar at 2 a.m., sat down by his box to offer him reassurance and the next thing I knew it was daylight, my left arm was numb and I was waking up with a dry mouth and my hair in a milk saucer.

This couldn't go on. The problem we had was that we lived in a typical Northumbrian cottage and typical Northumbrian cottages are one storeyed. That meant that even when we were in a separate room we were never more then a few yards from Ingemar. It was impossible to sleep through his tragic yelping, and even if it had been possible I'm not sure I'd have wanted to sleep through it. He was a baby. Strangers had taken him away from his mother and all that was familiar to him and plonked him down in a weird world full of peculiar things. No wonder he was disorientated and disturbed.

'What we'll do,' I said to Catherine, 'is we'll put his bed just outside our bedroom door and then we'll ever so gradually move it away, night by night, until it's in the kitchen. We're not weakening or disobeying our instruction sheet, we're just delivering the same result in a kinder and more subtle manner.'

After another sleepless night, I said, 'Well, maybe we could start with his bed in our room and gradually move it towards the door.'

For the next thirteen years Ingo slept in our bedroom.

It turned out that Little Man's early life had been chequered. He was the only pup in the litter – not so unusual in long-backed breeds. The breeder had sold him to a young couple but they had returned him, saying that he had bitten one of their children. The breeder pointed out that ten-week-old puppies bit everything, but the couple – who were plainly the sort of gormless morons the British dog-websites were trying to ward off with their ceaseless negativity – were adamant that they couldn't have a vicious dog in the house.

The breeder and her husband had then gone to Canada for two months to visit relatives and Manny had been sent to stay at the kennels of a friend of theirs who bred beagles. When they got back they had given Manny to their niece who helped them at shows. The idea was that Manny would be her own show dog. But at his first show the judge had pointed out a fault in the alignment of Manny's teeth that disqualified him from competition, and so they had decided not to keep him after all but to sell him as a pet instead. Then shortly after we went to see him, the breeder was taken seriously ill and Manny was sent to stay with the beagles again. When we agreed to buy him, it was the beagleman who brought him over to the house.

The beagleman dropped Manny off, said that the house, garden and location looked perfect for a dog, drank a quick cup of coffee and drove away. He didn't leave an instruction sheet. Not even a very minimal one.

After the beagleman had gone Manny ran frantically up and down the house, from one end to the other and back again. I took him for a walk on his new lead to try and settle him down but he was too distracted even to cock his leg. When we got back he started running up and down again pausing only to relieve himself on various bits of furniture. He'd been used to living out of doors in a pack. He was just over twelve months old. He'd never been without canine companionship in his life and he'd never been house-trained.

I tried feeding him. He wouldn't eat. I tried to interest him in various toys I had bought. He ignored them. Up and down he ran. By the time Catherine came home from work he was in a complete frenzy, his face matted with slather, eyes darting this way and that, and so unfocused it was as if he was crazed on drugs. When she bent down to try and pat him he jumped straight up at her and knocked her glasses off. He pooped on the carpet, he peed against the cast-iron stove so that steam came off it and condensed on the ceiling, he ran into Maisie's room, bit the head off a Bratz doll and barfed acid-yellow foam on her duvet. Round and round the house he ran. When we laid the table for tea he leapt up to try and grab a scone and pulled the tablecloth down sending crockery and food flying.

We phoned a friend of ours we knew had an unused dog cage. The breeder had said that all her dogs were used to going in a cage and we thought if he was in a confined space, one that he recognised, Little Man might calm down. My friend brought the cage over. We put Manny in it. He liked the cage, except when you shut the door. When you shut the door he flung himself against the mesh and howled. We let him out again. He ran to the other end of the house. Then he ran back and launched himself at our friend, striking him a painful blow in the groin. We asked our friend if he'd like a beer. He said that unfortunately it had just occurred to him that maybe he had left the cooker on and he thought he'd better go back and check.

Maisie had been at a birthday party and came home at 9 p.m. 'Where's the dog?' she shouted as she came through the door. Little Man sprinted from the far end of the house, sprang up at her at top speed and knocked her flat against the wall. His claws left scratch marks on her arm. She burst into tears and ran into her room. When she saw the decapitated doll she cried even louder. 'I don't think I want a dog after all,' she wailed. We shut her in her room as Manny continued to circle and leap. We tried closing various doors to limit him but when we did that he scrabbled madly at them, lacerating the paintwork.

At some point around 10 p.m. he briefly came to a halt, panting. I sat down beside him and stroked his head. 'Look,' I said, 'you've had a difficult start in life. You've been moved from one person to another. You've never had a settled place to live or a normal routine and you've never been taught anything. But you're here now and this is your home and it will be for the rest of your life. I give you my promise that you will live in this house for the rest of your life. I will not let you down.' This may seem quite an emotional speech to give to a dog but in truth it wasn't really Little Man I was attempting to reassure, it was myself. I lowered my head to look into his eyes. As I did so he darted forward and butted me so hard in the face that, for a moment, I thought he'd broken my nose.

Catherine and I had decided that I would sleep in the sitting room with Little Man for the first few nights until he was settled and could sleep in there on his own. 'He's not going to end up in the bedroom with us like Ingemar,' we said. Ingemar had been a noisy sleeping companion. He snored at a volume that lifted the duvet, yipped and twitched in his dreams, rustled round in his bed to get comfy and licked himself with such lip-smacking relish it sounded like somebody pulling a plunger off the face of a giant squid. His trumping was silent, at least, but the smell was so pungent it woke you up as surely as if you'd been slapped in the chops with a wet mop.

So I made a bed up on the floor, put Manny's beanbag nearby and, when everyone else was safely tucked up, shut the door and switched off the light. By now, Little Man was exhausted. I had watched him sitting in the

corner, his head gradually drooping, his eyes slowly closing, only for him to jerk himself awake again. He was
terrified of falling asleep: fearful of what might befall him
in this strange place if he did so. Even in the darkness, I
could hear him pacing about. I reached out when he came
near me and put my hand on his back. He was shivering
pathetically. I pulled him over next to me and stroked him
until he lay down. In kennels packs of basset griffon
Vendéen sleep tucked up so close to one another they look
like one homogeneous mass of fur. Now, Manny shoved his
head under my arm and tucked his nose under my chin
and, wrapped up like that, we both fell asleep.

We woke the next morning at 5.30. I got dressed and
walked Manny down the road and up through the wood
along the valley of a narrow stream. It was spring now
and the wild garlic was in flower, filling the air with its
savoury aroma. Goldfinches and yellowhammers hopped
about in the hawthorn bushes twittering, thrushes gur-
gled. We walked up Lamb Lane right to the top, where it
disappeared into the brown and boggy moor that
stretched up to Hadrian's Wall, and beyond to Kielder
Forest. We walked across the church field, heavy with dew,
the sun shining on the polished stone gravestones in the
churchyard so that they glowed orange, and back down
the lane for home. When we got back Catherine was
standing at the range boiling the kettle. I dried Manny's
feet and let him into the house. He scampered over to
Catherine, sat down in front of her, threw his head back
and delivered a pitch-perfect version of the basset griffon
yodel – 'Aaaaaaroooo!' – that we had listened to on the
Internet all those months before. And from then on everything was fine. More or less.

*

One afternoon, Manny and I bumped into Mr Fudgie down by the narrow path next to the river. That was not his real name, obviously. We didn't know what his real name was but his dog's name was Fudgie, so that is what we called him. Mr Fudgie and his family had moved to the village from the West Midlands. He had a strong Brummie accent. So strong, in fact, that for quite a while Catherine laboured under the misapprehension that his dog was called Food-Joy.

I first met Mr Fudgie very early one morning. Colour had not yet come into the world, the moon was hovering over the hills to the south like a mother-of-pearl gambling chip and I was walking along through the wood. I didn't usually encounter anyone when I went out at this time so I was surprised when we turned to head back home to find a man coming towards me. The man had a leggy young setter on a lunge line (usually used for horses). When they were about twenty yards from us Manny, who'd been busy sniffing after rabbits, suddenly saw them. He squeaked, darted into a thicket of ash saplings and began barking at the stranger.

'Sorry,' I said. 'We've only just got him and he's a bit nervous of other dogs.' At that moment there was a sudden gust of wind, followed by a loud crack and a large branch fell from a nearby beech tree and landed with a great thunk on the path between the setter-man and I. We both stared at the branch. It was ten feet long and heavy with leaves. I had dropped logs on my foot when carrying them in from the wood shed and I knew how much that hurt, so the thought of a piece of wood ten times the size falling from a far greater height on to my head didn't fill me with much enthusiasm. Suddenly the man with the setter burst out laughing. 'I think your dog must have had a premonition,' he said in his Brummie drone.

Mr Fudgie said he had never owned a dog before and had only really got this one so he could get out of the house and get some exercise. 'You feel funny just walking about on your own, don't you?' he said. I knew exactly what he meant. For a man in his thirties or forties, going for a walk in the countryside on his own is a bit problematic. People are either solicitous, or suspicious. Before we got Ingo I'd sometimes go for walks on my own. The trouble was when you strolled along the road some strangers stopped to offer you a lift in their car, while others hurriedly ushered their children indoors as you approached. Sometimes I'd walk several miles to post a letter, clutching the envelope in my hand so that observers knew I had a definite and legitimate purpose. A man out strolling with a dog looks natural. A man out walking alone looks sinister, or lost.

Mr Fudgie's dog was a bouncy Irish setter. To my mind, he was more caramel than fudge-coloured, but that would have been an altogether harder name to shout, so I didn't begrudge Mr Fudgie this touch of artistic licence. Fudgie was a rescue dog; he'd been found tied to a fence outside a big supermarket in Newcastle. 'No one knows how long he'd been there,' Mr Fudgie said. 'The dozy buggers who'd dumped him didn't even have the brains to make an anonymous call to the RSPCA and say where he was.' As a consequence, the Irish setter had issues. Most of them concerned food. He wouldn't let anyone go any-where near him when he was eating.

When I was a boy our family had acquired a West Highland terrier, Doogie. Doogie had suffered a bit as a pup. We'd got him when he was nearly a year old. He'd been locked in a shed at the bottom of someone's garden. They'd bought him for their little girl, the woman said, but when they had new fitted carpets laid he just made too much mess. Doogie had a thing about food too. He even growled at my mother if she went near him when he was at his dinner bowl, and he loved my mother. You could tell he didn't like doing it because he alternated between snarling and looking sheepish. He was compelled, yet ashamed of his compulsion. He'd bite you but as soon as he'd done it you could sense his embarrassment, which wasn't much compensation when you were having the tetanus jabs.

The big problem for us with Doogie was that our family lived in one of two farm cottages that been knocked into one. Like most former tied houses they had been expanded over the years in an altogether haphazard manner. Bits of our attic stuck out of over the neighbour's bedroom. Our hall was under her bathroom.

In the centre of the downstairs part of our house there was a kind of square about three feet across that formed the junction between the downstairs loo, the kitchen, the living room and the corridor that led to the front door. This square basically controlled entry to and from everything in the house, and for some reason it was here that Doogie had picked as the perfect spot to take any bone, or biscuit he was given. Once he was in there it was impossible to shift him. He'd lie over his catch and snarl whenever anybody went within two yards of him. And he wasn't just making a show either.

One afternoon, old Mrs Maynard from down the road called in to see my mother. Mrs Maynard used to call round every Sunday afternoon to play cards with our family and her neighbour old Mrs Smith. Mrs Maynard was a retired seaside landlady from Whitby and, in the days before anyone had even heard of the sporting phrase 'mind games', she was already an expert in them.

Mrs Maynard's opening psychological gambit was simplicity itself. She would pick another player at random, fix them with a gimlet eye and bark, 'Have you shinnied?' Inevitably this would provoke a back-and-forth of denial and allegation.

'Why would I shinny? I hate it when people shinny.'

'Well, that goes without saying. Nevertheless, you could have shinnied *in error*.'

The argument was pretty much irresolvable because the fact of the matter was that nobody else sitting round the table was quite sure what shinnying actually involved. My father believed that it was illegal playing of a trump card while, for my part, I have never been able to shake the feeling that it was actually a euphemism for farting.

After that diversion Mrs Maynard would begin her campaign to break all resistance using the cunning mental ploy of talking about her latest operation. The story would be as long and winding as the intestines that so often featured in it, but the culmination was always perfectly timed to coincide with the key moment of the game.

As the decisive hand was being played Mrs Maynard would wind up her tale. 'And you know what that surgeon said to me? He said, "Mrs Maynard, in thirty years in the medical profession I have never come across anything like it. It was,"' and she would pause at this point to survey the table, '"a solid wall of compacted matter."'

I don't care if you're Sir Alex Ferguson or Muhammad Ali I'd defy anyone to cope with that.

Anyway, on this occasion, having found nobody to terrorise over the card table, Mrs Maynard had had a cup of tea, given a detailed rundown on her latest gastric complaint, her last barium meal and the colour of her bile and then popped into the lavatory. At this point my granddad arrived and gave Doogie a dog chew. Mrs Maynard was trapped in the toilet for well over an hour. At one point we thought we were going to have to pull her out through the half-light.

In fairness to Doogie, it should be said that he was only possessive over food that was given to him. Mr Fudgie's dog was much more difficult. Fudgie was proactive. If he was left alone in a room with food he assumed it was his. 'Last Sunday, the wife put the beef joint up on the counter to rest and went off to powder her nose. When she came back buggerlugs here wouldn't let her in the kitchen.'

'What did you do?' I asked.

'Went down the pub,' Mr Fudgie said. 'Four slices of Northumbrian lamb, six different vegetables, yorkies, and apple pie to finish and all for £6.50 a head. It's not bad, is it?'

Mr Fudgie was addressing the problem of Fudgie's food obsession. 'I've been taking him to see an animal psychologist,' he said.

I imagined an office with Turkish rugs and wood-panelled walls covered with framed certificates. At one side, a little man in a tweed suit with a goatee beard and round spectacles sits in a leather chesterfield beside a large oak desk. He greets the patient. 'Welcome, Fudgie. I hope you are well. Now, if you'd just like to make yourself comfortable on the couch,' and Mr Fudgie says, 'Oh no, mate, he's not allowed on the furniture.'

Mr Fudgie said the psychologist was helping identify Fudgie's problems, which all stemmed from the traumas of his puppyhood. Mr Fudgie got very cross about the way Fudgie had been treated by his previous owners. 'If they'd treat a dog like that I hate to think how they must treat their kids,' he said. To somebody that isn't a dog owner that might seem like a strange thing to say, but I understood where Mr Fudgie was coming from. A pedigree dog like Fudgie would have cost about £500; you get children for free. And you don't have to pay for their inoculations either.

'They are out there now and I bet they don't feel so much as a smidgeon of guilt,' Mr Fudgie said. It was the angriest I would ever see him. Mr Fudgie was generally a droll and self-deprecating fellow. Things always seemed to go wrong for him but he always turned them into a joke. Whenever I saw him I thought of the old Les Dawson gag: 'I'm so unlucky the other day I peeled a banana and it was empty.'

Once, he told me about a visit he'd made to the Moët & Chandon chateau in France. He and his workmates had been taken on a tour of the famous champagne vineyards and afterwards they'd had an elaborate dinner in the main dining hall of the castle. 'Beautiful, it was,' Mr Fudgie said. 'Crystal chandeliers, gilded candelabra, lace tablecloths, waiting staff all in golden livery.' They had eaten seven courses, each accompanied by a different champagne. 'Absolutely superb,' Mr Fudgie said. 'And then, when we were having coffee and a glass of fifty-year-old eau de vie, one of the footmen came round with a mahogany box filled with Cuban cigars.

'Well, I've always liked a cigar, so I helped myself, didn't I?' Mr Fudgie said. 'But when I looked at it I was a bit puzzled because I was only really used to slim panatellas and Wintermans Café Crèmes, and I'd never seen a cigar that was round at both ends. By then we'd sunk a fair bit of stuff and, as I looked at this cigar, I was suddenly struck by an inspiration. I'd never seen one like it in real life, but I'd seen them at the pictures – in cowboy films. And when

Clint Eastwood or John Wayne took out a cigar they always did the same thing – bit the end off it. So I thought that's what I'd do.

'Well, I tell you mate,' Mr Fudgie said, 'it's not half as easy as Clint makes it look, biting the end off a cigar. I had a go, but instead of coming away cleanly it sort of tore and all these long strands of tobacco started to pull out of it.'

At this point Mr Fudgie heard a polite cough behind him. 'I turned around,' he said, 'with this cigar end in my gob, and all the strands of tobacco hanging down my chin and there was this imperious liveried butler offering me a pair of silver secateurs.'

It turned out that Mrs Pelham-Beale was president of the local Women's Institute. One day the phone rang. I picked up. 'Hairy Pee'son?' an unmistakable voice roared down the line. I was quite pleased I had placed the receiver to my right ear as I'd gone a little deaf in my left and, at the first word from Mrs Pelham-Beale, the ball of wax that had been blocking it pinged straight out and splattered on the wall. 'You the rider?' she continued. I affirmed that I was.

'Talk. WI. September 22nd, 7.30. Do it?'

I said I could. In fact, I'd be delighted.

''Spect you thought we'd all be naked!' Mrs Pelham-Beale barked jovially when I was seated in front of the fifteen or so elderly ladies who made up the local WI membership. This was a reference to the WI calendar that had just come out showing members from Cumbria in the nude (it would later inspire the film *Calendar Girls* starring Dame Helen Mirren). Mrs Pelham-Beale's remark would have been quite funny, except that at that point I had not heard about the Cumbrian WI's pin-up calendar. Instead of making me laugh, therefore, it just made me feel very, very uneasy.

The WI was founded by a Canadian woman at the tail end of the nineteenth century to teach mothers about health and hygiene. Now they were torch-bearers for amateur glamour modelling. They had sparked a trend. These days nude calendars are all the rage across rural Britain. In the autumn you can hardly open the local paper without finding a picture of a grinning gamekeeper with only a brace of grouse hiding his vitals, or the head of the knitting circle, wearing nothing but three balls of mohair and a saucy grin, under a headline reading: 'Local Folk Shed Clothes To Raise Funds'. The exhibitionism is all in a good cause, you see (though obviously that depends on whether you consider field sports or the Country Landowners Association a good cause). At one time in rural Britain raising money for charity generally involved cross-dressing. Young Farmers, Rotarians, the police, the Conservative and Unionist clubs, if they wanted the public to stump up cash invariably did it by stuffing two balloons up their T-shirts, putting on some fishnet tights and singing something by Madonna. Now they take their togs off instead. In the countryside nudity is the new transvestism.

I was pleased to be asked to attend the WI meeting because it has long been my contention that an English man or woman who craves entry into a world of the mysterious and bizarre is faced with a simple choice. You can fly to a distant rainforest, paddle up a piranha-stuffed river, hack through snake-infested jungle and then spend a few months with the sort of folk who manufacture a potent alcoholic drink by chewing up leaves and spitting them into a hollow tree; or you can stay at home, buy the local paper and read the WI reports. ('Members and visitors enjoyed a lively beetle drive followed by pie and peas supper. The prize for the best everyday object shaped like a stoat was won by Mrs Dawkins.')

I put this point to a Women's Institute meeting. It was greeted, as I suspected it might be, with wry chuckles. As the nude-calendar incident showed, WI members have a keen sense of irony. Besides which, you never get much argument when you suggest to English people that they are, perhaps, just a little eccentric. It is the equivalent of telling a Frenchman he's wonderful.

Not that you need confine your search for strangeness to the WI. The British countryside is full of arcane and bewildering things. Try entering one of the baking competitions at the local agricultural show. They are always housed in the Industrial Tent, a coincidence that says far more about the English attitude to food than a thousand TV cookery programmes. The Industrial Tent is a place of wonder, containing all the culinary arts at which the English excel: cakes, jam, pies, chutney, and animals made out of vegetables. It's also the place where extraordinary rituals, the origins and meanings of which nobody can explain, are played out. Why, for example, do show committees of the Industrial Section (Home Baking) insist that scones are entered in fours, while eclairs and meringues need only come in triplicate and a pair of teacakes is considered quite sufficient? Is there some socio-economic reason why biscuits in North Yorkshire must be entered by the half dozen, while just four suffice in County Durham? Yet, while nobody is clear why iced buns must be 'in paper wrappers', or the coconut haystacks must be 'egg-cup sized', one thing is certain: you ignore the instructions at your peril. Disqualification and ignominy await those who transgress The Code.

Nowadays, the WI runs a course in baking etiquette to avoid such sticky situations. 'I remember the first show I entered,' one member confessed as we sat over our tea and dainties at the meeting's end (my talk on country fairs had gone down well and I had successfully negotiated the tricky task of judging the 'most unusual teaspoon' contest). 'I was ruled ineligible because I'd crimped my sausage rolls instead of concealing the seams.'

'Were they shortcrust?' the woman sitting next to her asked. 'Because you never crimp shortcrust. It's like a savoury quiche; if you were to enter a savoury quiche in a fluted dish you would be disqualified.'

'Why?' I asked.

'Because,' the speaker said matter-of-factly, 'only a sweet flan should be fluted, of course.'

Well, obviously.

April

Walking along Hadrian's Wall with some friends and their children we met two women with a three-legged Labrador. Manny and the Labrador exchanged greetings. 'Your dog's only got three legs,' the youngest of the children announced to one of the women.

'Yes, I noticed,' the woman said with a chuckle.

'How did it happen?' the boy asked.

'Well,' the woman said, 'a few years ago she got a growth in her knee and they had to cut it off.'

'Does she mind?'

'I'm sure she'd rather she had all four,' the woman said, 'but she doesn't complain, do you, Sophie?' Sophie looked up at her with mournful gundog eyes. She reminded me of the first dog I ever knew.

Sam our cocker spaniel lived a rather idyllic life. It was back in the 1960s, there were very few cars on the road and our village wasn't en route to anywhere. In the morning, my mum would put Sam out and go off to work and in the late afternoon when she came back she'd bang a spoon on his dinner bowl a few times and he would appear from the river bank at the bottom of the garden and come sprinting across the lawn.

We never knew what he got up to during the day, but it was clear that he ranged around a fair bit. Occasionally we'd meet people when we were out for walks and they'd say, 'Oh, is that chap yours? We wondered where he came from. He turns up on our doorstep, regular as clockwork, every Tuesday at 11 a.m. We give him a rich tea biscuit and off he trots.' Sometimes the people who said these types of things lived nearby, sometimes they lived at the bottom end of the village and once or twice they lived in different villages altogether. What we could glean from these meetings was that Sam plotted a fairly regular course over the five days of the working week, moving to some plan and rhythm in his head that would forever be a mystery to us.

The years went by and Sam continued his happy wandering. One day when he was off on his travels my father decided to do some building work in the garden. We'd had a kitchen extension built and the stone steps that came down from the lawn no longer led directly to the back door. My father removed the old steps, filled the gap with stone and turf and put the new steps in four yards to the left of where they had been previously. The job was executed with remarkably little incident. This was not always the case with my father. He was a meticulously neat and methodical worker who treated his tools and materials with the utmost respect but extended little thought to his own physical well-being. If my father was using a hammer you could more or less guarantee he would hit himself with it. Counting the number of times he nailed his boots to planks of wood would have required the fingers of both his hands, one of which was bound to be bandaged following an earlier incident with a hacksaw. Sometimes my father displayed such cavalier disdain for his own safety I wondered if he wasn't joyriding in a stolen body.

Relieved that a piece of DIY had for once passed off without blood and stitches my mother served tea in the garden. 'Where's Sam?' I asked.

'He'll be around,' my mother said and she picked up his dinner bowl and struck it three times with a cold chisel. Sure enough Sam came bundling up the garden at full tilt, ran straight to where the steps had once been and fell straight off the edge, landing in a confused mewling heap on the paving below. My mother rushed over to him.

'I wonder why he did that,' my father said scratching at a splinter in his thumb.

My mother picked Sam up and looked at his face as if for the first time. 'I think,' she said, after studying it for a while, 'that he is blind.' And she was right.

Exactly when Sam had lost his sight we could never establish, but it had clearly been some while before the incident with the steps. Yet he had gone on trundling round his circuit as if nothing had been amiss. 'A dog never complains,' my mother said. 'He doesn't moan. He just accepts his lot and gets on with things as best he can. When it comes to attitude, people could learn a lot from dogs.'

I came across Mr Fudgie down where the old mill-race rushed through a stand of pine trees. It had been raining steadily for several days and the fields, filled with newly sprung wheat and barley, had taken on the look of rice paddies. Water glistened between the green rows and herons stalked through them looking for frogs and fleeing field mice.

A dipper was standing on a rock near the bank,

bobbing repeatedly at the knees. There was something anxious about the dipper. With his dark back and wings and white throat, he looked like a Victorian gentleman in evening dress who, on presentation to the Queen, had got into a terrible funk and was curtseying instead of bowing.

The sight of all the water had made Mr Fudgie nostalgic. He said he had done a foolish thing when he first got Fudge. He had taken the setter down to the river and, as soon as it saw the water, the dog had sprinted forward and plunged straight in. There had been snow and it had melted that week, Mr Fudgie said. The river was high and the minute Fudge hit the water he had been swept away. Mr Fudgie had run along the bank until he was level with the dog and then he had jumped in to save it. 'I don't know what came over me,' Mr Fudgie said. 'I must have gone mental. The minute I hit the water and felt it rising up past my knees, my thighs, my waist, my belly button, I said to myself, "You bloody idiot. Now you're going to be one of those people on the news who drowns trying to save a dog." And you know how those stories always end . . .'

'The dog is later found unharmed further downstream,' I said.

'Exactly,' Mr Fudgie said. As it was, he had felt the river-bed below his feet when the water was just past his chest and, with considerable effort, had succeeded in hauling himself back onto the bank. 'I was wet through and bloody freezing,' he said, 'lying there exhausted, like a beached whale, and suddenly I feel buggerlugs here licking my face.'

'He was found unharmed further downstream,' I said.

Mr Fudgie said he hoped that was the only time he came close to featuring in a dog-related news snippet.

'Because there's one other one that always makes my blood run cold when I hear it,' he said.

'I know the one,' I said. '"The body was discovered early this morning by a man out walking his dog."'

Mr Fudgie pulled a face and shivered; 'Yep,' he said. 'That's the one.'

When I walked Little Man along the river this morning I heard the call of a cuckoo. It was the first time I had ever heard one in Northumberland. Like grey squirrels, Sainsbury's and caffè latte, *Cuculus canorus* had been gradually edging northwards over the last few decades. This was good news for fans of biodiversity, but bad news for the local small birds who were likely to find themselves with one large extra mouth to feed.

As a man with a vague commitment to rationality I had always put myself firmly in the camp of those who believe in evolution, but no matter how hard I pondered I could never quite work out how the cuckoo had arrived at its chosen survival strategy: laying its eggs in other birds' nests. The only theory I could come up with was that it had originally happened by accident. One day a female cuckoo, homeless and alone, having been cruelly used and discarded by the notoriously dashing yet unscrupulous male of the species, sought sanctuary in the nest of a chaffinch, laid her eggs and then, lest shame and opprobrium be rained down upon her by censorious starlings and jays, fled the scene of her disgrace. Weeks later, wracked by guilt, she returned to see what had become of her infant and was surprised to discover that the chaffinches had not – as she had fully expected – turned her baby over to the tender mercies of the social services but were bringing the gargantuan child up as their own.

Soon her discovery was the talk of all the pavement cafes/bars where fashionable career cuckoos meet. 'Apparently they take care of the infant marvellously well and absolutely refuse any recompense whatsoever.'

'Free childcare! My God, it's like Sweden or something!'

Maybe this was what happened, but it still didn't explain how the system benefited the cuckoo. OK, the male and female saved lots of time and energy by farming out the parenting to third parties, but what exactly did they do with it? Work as barristers? Set up an antique shop? Go clubbing? There was no evidence of any of this. Indeed, aside from prompting retired colonels from the home counties to write a letter to *The Times* every April, the cuckoos seemed to make only the most limited contribution to society.

And then there were the foster parents. If, as seemed likely, the cuckoos had been palming off their eggs on finches, pipits and warblers for centuries, how come no bird had ever rumbled their little scheme? It isn't as if birds aren't intelligent. We know that from the milk business. Up until the 1920s British milkmen delivered milk in bottles without lids and blue tits and robins all helped themselves to the fatty cream on the top as the bottles sat on the doorstep. Then the milkmen started to put foil caps on the bottles and for two decades milk disappeared from the avian diet. Sometime in the late 1950s, however, it was reported that blue tits in south-west England had started pecking through the foil. Soon, in a prime example of culturally transmitted learning, blue tits across Britain were doing the same thing. Oddly, though, the message has never got through to robins. Ornithologists say that this is because the blue tit is a flock bird, whereas the robin is territorial. I think there is a good deal of truth in that. The robin has always struck me as a rather arrogant little blighter. Whenever I was digging the garden a robin would come and watch me. He had the beady look in his eye of a country landowner keeping tabs on a shiftless tenant farmer. 'Look there's our robin,' Catherine would sometimes say when he appeared.

And I thought, 'He's not *our* robin, we're *his* humans.'

Robins were macho fellows and I'm sure that explained why the news about the foil tops never spread amongst them. Like any red-blooded (or indeed red-breasted) male, the robin would be reluctant to share any hard-won knowledge, preferring instead to keep it to himself and strut around showing off.

Be that as it may, or may not, the fact is that if small birds could fathom out something like this and then tell all their friends about it, how come they had never sussed out what the cuckoos were up to?

Clearly you wouldn't have expected the actual surrogate parents to notice. Like all mums and dads of small children, the birds with the cuckoo in their nests would simply be too tired to notice. When you have a small child you rely on your friends to point things out to you: 'Er, did you know you've got egg in your hair/milky sick down your back/your underpants on inside out and over the top of your trousers?' That sort of thing.

In this case, though, pointing out the obvious was maybe just too embarrassing even for the birds' oldest chums. 'Well, I am sorry, Jocasta, but that big one in the middle looks absolutely nothing like Gerald. Are you sure you've been faithful to him?' In the end I guess they just decided not to say anything.

I can't be sure about that, of course, but one thing was certain to me. And that was that when the adolescent cuckoo finally did leave the nest he did so in an almighty huff, cooing, 'I hate you! You're not my real parents' at the selfless meadow pipits who had raised him.

I was so busy following this convoluted train of thought that I barely noticed Mr Dodds approaching, dragging Taffy behind him. 'Heard yon cuckoo?' he asked. I said I had.

'How come the other birds don't notice when it lays its egg in their nest?' I asked.

Mr Dodds wrinkled up his nose. 'To be honest I've never given it much thought,' he said. 'Have you?'

'No,' I said. 'No, not really.'

'Lovely being out when the sun's first on the water,' the fisherman said cheerfully as Manny and I passed by on the bank. This was quite a surprise. Most fishermen did not say anything. They just stood gazing morosely at the water like alcoholics staring into the first drink of the day. And that was if you were lucky.

Every once in a while, when I was elsewhere in the North-East, I'd tell the fellow I was talking to where I lived and he'd raise an eyebrow and say, 'Bit of a rough spot that, isn't it?' At first I couldn't work out how the village had got such a reputation, but then it dawned on me that all the people who thought the place I lived in was a haven for nutters and yahoos were anglers.

You see, there was a bitter and long-running dispute over local fishing rights on the river. It had all boiled down to a legal battle between the British Rail Angling Club (the business of British Rail may have been dismantled by Mrs Thatcher, but the Iron Lady never got her hands on the social side of it), who claimed that because the train track ran alongside the river the bank too belonged to them, and the local angling club, who felt that since the river bank was in their village it was theirs. As the stretch of river offered some of the best salmon fishing in England neither side would back down.

The matter was pursued through solicitors at immense cost – the angling club's fees rose year on year, more or less entirely to cover the legal bills – and tempers became increasingly frayed. At one point Tucker threatened to sue Rail Track for compensation after Tadger the terrier got covered in the axle grease and had to go to the local poodle parlour and have his fur cut off. The axle grease had been smeared all over the pole of a sign that proclaimed: 'Private Fishing. British Rail Angling Club'.

The axle grease, it should be noted, had only been smeared on the pole after the sign had been uprooted several times and chucked in the river. Although I should add that this sign had only been thrown in the river after the original sign that read 'Private Fishing', followed by the name of the local angling club, had been sprayed over with black paint.

After a volley of letters from Tommy, some workmen from whatever branch of what was once British Rail that now dealt with such matters came and removed the axle grease from the pole. Twenty-four hours later the sign was back in the river again. And so it went on. There were reports of fights and beatings, and quite often the men who said, 'A bit of a rough place that, isn't it?' would add, 'They torched one lad's car.' Though I had no idea whether that was true or not, it was a clear indication of just how stupid things had become.

Implausible though these tales may seem to an outsider, I didn't find it impossible to believe them. A lot of fishermen seem to teeter permanently on the cusp of outrage.

As a boy I spent much of my school holidays running away from them after my friends and I had 'frightened the fish' by throwing stones at floating bottles, jumping about on the bank, or simply standing quietly licking our lollypops. Basically, fishermen don't want anybody but other fishermen anywhere near a river.

Once my friend Andy – the one who almost named his cat Steve – and I had gone in to one of the local pubs on a Sunday lunchtime. We'd walked in and it was raining and Andy was wearing a blue kagoul. As we ate our sandwiches the barmaid came over and, leaning over conspiratorially, asked, 'Are you lads canoeists?'

We told her we weren't canoeists, we were pedestrians. 'Oh, that's good,' she said, the relief in her voice palpable. 'Only, those lads over there are fishermen and they don't like canoeists. Frighten the fish, you see.' We watched as she left us, walked over to a group of men standing near the bar and said something to them. The men nodded, then the biggest of them looked over in our direction, grinned and gave us a heads up. We went away with the distinct impression we'd narrowly avoided a good pummelling.

Personally, I couldn't see what was worth getting so worked up about. But then I don't like fishing. When I want to spend hour upon hour in the fresh air watching very little happen I go to a cricket match. There is beer at that, too. Though, of course, you don't get to wear thigh-length rubber boots.

My father was a keen angler and when I was a teenager he tried to induct me into the brotherhood of lure and live bait. 'Now,' my father would say as we stood in the drizzle on some shingle bank alongside the River Leven, 'in order to catch a fish you must think like a fish. If you were a fish what would you be thinking?'

'How do I burp underwater,' I replied. It's a wonder he never drowned me, really.

My father was not obsessed by fishing, though many people are. Sporting obsession is generally seen as a male trait: nature's compensation for the long hours men must pass between our brief intervention in the perpetuation of the species and inevitable death. If this is the case then it is perhaps fitting that sporting obsession in its purest form should be found in the size-fixated world of angling.

However, it seems that when it comes to bigness British freshwater fish cannot match up to their overseas counterparts. That is what led to the introduction of rainbow trout into British rivers back in the 1950s. The North American fish were tougher and grew faster than the native brown trout. But that was only the start. Recently it has been reported that unscrupulous anglers have taken to smuggling gigantic fish from abroad, so they can catch them later, break records and get their pictures in the angling magazines next to the adverts for waders and maggots. Carp and catfish – mud-dwelling beasts with the drooping moustaches of 1970s detectives – are the most popular breeds of contraband.

In China, meanwhile, the quest for ever bigger fish has taken an even more sinister turn. Scientists have boosted the growth rate of the common carp by up to 20 per cent, producing monsters that weigh as much as 150 lb (ten times the British record). They do this by implanting the carp with cattle genes. What the effect this tampering will have on the physical appearance of the carp is not yet known. Though it is possible that in a few years' time fishermen will be standing on the riverbank armed not with a rod and keep net but a sword and matador's cape.

*

Rain was forecast for later in the day and the farmers had seized the opportunity to do some muck-spreading. The sickly sweet smell of slurry hung over the fields. The day was warm but all the windows in the village were shut tight and the washing lines were empty. 'Take a deep breath. It's good for your lungs,' my grandmother would say whenever we passed a field where the muck-spreader had been in action. My granny was full of such ancient country wisdom. Sitting on a cold step gave you piles; sucking sugar lumps gave you worms; an earwig would crawl in through your ear hole at night and munch your brains; eating burned toast made your hair curly. Quite often these days I hear people on the radio or on TV complaining that modern medicine ignores traditional remedies and that centuries of accumulated folk learning have been lost as a result. Whenever I hear anyone talking like that I think of my grandmother, and breathe a sigh of relief.

One of my grandmother's many pieces of folk wisdom was that 'if a bat flies into your hair it gets so tangled up in it you have to have it all shaved off *with a razor*'. I'm not sure from what branch of the family this eldritch saw had been handed down, though it's possible she had just made it up to deter me and my friend 'Turnip' Turner from what had become our favourite evening pastime – standing in the back alley behind her house and throwing our jumpers up at bats in the hope of catching one. If this was the case her efforts were wasted because we carried on regardless. And no matter how long we delayed our throw, waiting almost until the bat was above our heads before chucking our jumpers, or how accurately we placed them in its apparent flight path, the bat always jinked aside at the last split second to avoid them.

Whatever the motivation or origins of the 'bat in the hair' tale, I now know from personal experience that it is not true because one night when I took Little Man out for his final pee-parade of the day a bat flew round the corner of the neighbour's house just as I was approaching it from the opposite direction and smacked straight into the top of my head. It didn't get caught in my hair. It simply bounced off and flew on.

This was my second close encounter with a common pipistrelle in the space of a fortnight. The first had not been quite so brief, or decisive. It was a warm spring evening and we had one of the windows open in the sitting room. When Catherine went to close it later on she found a bat circling the room. She shut the door and came and found me in my office. 'We'll have to let it out,' she said.

Since Catherine hides under the duvet in terror whenever a moth enters the room it was plain exactly who 'we' was on this occasion. I went out into the corridor and peeped in through the sitting room door. The bat was still flying round and round the central light fitting. 'What I'll do,' I said to Catherine, 'is I'll crawl across the floor and open the front door and the other window and switch off the light and then come back. And we'll shut this door and leave it for a few hours and it will fly off.'

'Why will you crawl?' Catherine asked.

'Because it might fly into me if I walk,' I said.

'No, it won't,' Catherine said. 'They send out those sonar signals; they never collide with anything. They squeak and it echoes back to them off solid objects. There was a programme about it on Radio Four.'

'Yes, I know all that,' I said. 'But . . . well . . . you know. If they get in your hair it can be very nasty.'

'Who told you that?' Catherine asked.

'My granny,' I said.

'And you believe it?'

'No, obviously I don't believe it. I think it's nonsense. But there's a big difference between not believing in something theoretically and not believing in it when, if you're wrong, you could end up with a horrible leathery flying rodent flapping about on your head.'

'I think you're being a bit melodramatic,' Catherine said.

'And this,' I retorted, 'from somebody who comes shrieking out of the bathroom because there's an insect in there the size of a postage stamp.'

'Moths flap in your face. They get in behind your glasses.'

'I'm crawling,' I said. 'Either that or we can stand here talking until it's time for the bat to hibernate.'

So I opened the door slowly and then slithered across the carpet commando-style. When I got to the other side of the room I slowly rose to a crouching position and opened the front door. Then I slithered along the wall, reached up and opened the rest of the windows, switched off the light and crawled back to the corridor.

After some merriment at my expense we went and did a few things and when it was time to go to bed we peeped into the sitting room. The bat was nowhere to be seen. 'It's gone,' I said. I went in and shut the doors and windows, turned around and there was the bat, flying in circles around the light fitting. I crawled back to the corridor. 'What we'll do is,' I said, 'switch off the light, shut this door and leave it in there. In the morning we can open all the windows again and it will go then. Manny can sleep in our room tonight.'

We went to bed. Ten minutes passed then suddenly
Manny ran out into the corridor and started barking.
'What's the matter with you? Come back here,' I said.
But Manny ignored me and kept on barking. I went out to
get him. He was up on his hind legs, barking at something
above him. As I stepped out into the corridor the bat flew
straight past my ear. 'Jesus Christ!' I yelled, hauling
Manny back into the bedroom by his collar and slam-
ming the door behind me. 'It's out there!' I said to
Catherine. 'It's got through the sitting room door.'

'Maybe it flew out when you were crawling around,'
Catherine said. I said that was impossible. 'The door was
only open a few seconds. We'd have seen it.'

'Maybe it's not the same bat,' Catherine said.

'You're saying there's more than one in the house?
What is this, a bat invasion? I'm beginning to feel like
Rod Taylor in *The Birds*.'

It was a feeling that increased a few seconds later when
Manny suddenly leapt at the bottom of the bedroom door
yelping excitedly. I pulled him away, looked down and
there was the bat squeezing itself under the door, dragging
itself forward using the claws on the front of its wings, its
little mouth opening and closing with the effort.

'Oh no!' I shouted.

'What on earth's the matter?' Catherine said. I didn't
need to answer because at that moment the bat popped
up from under the door, took off and flew across the
room.

'It must be attracted by the light,' Catherine said, after
we had both crawled out of the bedroom, shut the door
behind us and stuffed a towel under the bottom of the
door to prevent the bat following us.

'I think you're right,' I said. 'But I don't get it? Why are nocturnal creatures always attracted to light? If they like light so much why don't they come out in the day when there's plenty of it and they could have their fill without bothering people?'

We spent the night on the sitting room floor. When we went into the bedroom the next day the bat had gone.

May

Manny and I walked up the hill towards the fell. An RAF Hercules passed low overhead, flying down the river valley. The big transport plane made the same droning noise as the cockchafers that had lately been battering out a ponderous rhythm on our windows in the evening. After half an hour I'd go out and there would be two dozen of them lying on their backs on the concrete path, their legs frantically pedalling the air. I like May bugs, there is something endearing about their comical bulk, so I'd tip them all upright. And half-an-hour later I'd go out and do it again.

Spring was in full spate now. Birds were singing merrily, lambs were bleating and the grass was so green it practically hurt your eyes to look at it. It reminded me that the artist James Whistler had once complained that nature was far too strident to please the aesthete.

I stood watching some bullfinches bumping about amongst the blossom of a blackthorn bush. Every time I see a male bullfinch I think of the one in the Saki short story that whistles an air from *Iphigénie en Tauride* and 'fancied himself something of a despot'. With his puffed out chest, beady eyes and gaudy plumage there is certainly something of the military ruler about him, you can imagine him strutting down the garden path waving a wing at admiring crowds without ever deigning to actually look at them.

Just before we turned into a green lane that ran up by a stand of larches, Jasper the binman came round the corner carrying an air rifle and a couple of dead grey squirrels. The greys had only just started to appear in Northumberland. For years the Tyne had held them at bay and we'd been able to watch red squirrels cavorting about in the pine trees at the bottom of the garden, but six months before I had seen a grey scurrying along the top of the wall near the church. I felt like a Saxon sighting his first Viking longship. The consequences were equally inevitable: soon the greys were everywhere and the reds had vanished.

There was talk of eradicating the invader, but people had been saying that practically since the first Canadian grey squirrels had been let loose in Cheshire back in 1876. In 1932 the Forestry Commission had started paying a bounty of sixpence (2½p) per tail. In the 1940s the government had introduced a policy of extermination offering one shilling (5p) or two shotgun cartridges per corpse. By the early 1960s the price on a grey squirrel's tail had risen to five shillings (25p). It did no good. The greys bred too rapidly and spread too fast to be controlled. Nowadays nobody knows how many there are in Britain. You can get some idea though by looking at the mainland European equivalent of the grey squirrel, the muskrat. The Habsburgs introduced the muskrat from North America as a source of fur back in 1906. Five breeding pairs were released in Austro-Hungary. By 1926 there were muskrats across most of the continent, estimates say as many as 100 million. Even the coypu, a large South American rodent that escaped from East Anglian fur farms back in the 1930s and took up residence in the fens, has managed to thrive in its new environment. From the late 1970s to the mid 1980s trappers working for the ministry of agriculture killed 35,000 of them. And the coypu is a native of the Amazon rainforest. It dies when it gets cold. The grey squirrel has no such problems with the British climate.

Since guns and traps had failed those wanting to protect the red squirrel from the invasive grey, they were turning to other methods. Recently one of the leading lights in the Forestry Commission had suggested that contraception was the answer.

I mentioned this to Jasper.

'Well,' he said, scratching his chin thoughtfully. 'It sounds like a good plan, but I can't help wondering who is going to teach the squirrels how to put the contraceptives on.'

Jasper was not much older than me but years of outdoor living had weathered his skin to the texture of alder bark and blown all the colour out of his sideburns and whiskers. In the past when I'd met him he had nearly always been in the company of his teenage son but, like the red squirrels, the lad too seemed to have disappeared lately. I asked Jasper how his son was getting on. 'I hardly see him these days,' Jasper replied.

'Parties, rock concerts and girls?' I suggested.

'No,' he said. 'Beating, stalking and ferreting.'

The last time I saw the juvenile in question he was wearing a hoodie that bore the slogan 'Vote For Satan', so I like to believe he will be taking a slightly more rock 'n' roll approach to deer stalking than is traditional. Instead of simply following the doe in the usual manner across crag and forest in plus fours and a hat with two peaks, I imagine he is sitting in one of those bars that serves Chardonnay in pint glasses bombarding her with obscene text messages: 'U R Horny' and that sort of thing. What I think about the beating and ferreting I will keep to myself.

Whatever Jasper the binman's son gets up to on moor and fell, the very presence of somebody who doesn't think The Darkness is a popular nickname for the Labour Party is surely something for which field sports have been crying out. The whole practice of mangling wild animals needs to be dragged into the twenty-first century (preferably by a pack of large and savage dogs) and the first step in doing so is surely acquiring the sort of 'bad boy' character that – like Eric Cantona or Dennis Rodman – can cross over and appeal to the disaffected youths of the marketing departments of major sportswear brands around the world. If they can pull it off there could be a fortune in it, and in future our shopping malls will be filled with teenagers loafing round in Harris tweed plus fours, Norfolk jackets and stout brogans.

Jasper said he was a bit depressed, to be honest. Not only was his attempt to hold back the advancing tide of grey squirrels proving futile but now he had been forced to move his beehives as well. When I had first met him he had some in the wood at the bottom of our garden. I'd asked him a few questions about beekeeping one afternoon and, sensing a possible convert to apiary, he had offered to supply me with 'everything you need to get started'.

'Do you get immune to the sting?' I asked hopefully.

Jasper shrugged, 'No,' he replied, 'But you get used to them after the first dozen or so.'

I wasn't sure I wanted to get used to being stung by bees. It reminded me of the old joke about the man who comes across a chap hitting himself repeatedly on the forehead with a mallet. 'Why are you doing that?' he asks.

'Because it feels so good when I stop,' the man replies. I turned down the beehive.

Other people clearly had similar feelings. 'I had to move them,' Jasper said. 'They were near the house, you know, and the bees kept stinging people. Sam the postman, they stung him. Jocky the postman, they stung him. The lad from Parcelforce, they stung him. The DHL courier, they stung him. The electric-metre man, they stung him. The gadgie from the waterboard, they stung him. The old wifey who brings the Parish magazine, they stung her. The lad who delivers the gas . . . now, I mind they didn't sting him.' He pondered a moment. 'No, when I think about it, they stung him an' all.'

Jasper had a lot of chickens running loose in the garden outside his house where the beehives had once stood. When we'd first noticed them I had asked Jasper if we could buy some eggs off him. 'I can't sell eggs on account of the European Union Health and Safety Directive,' Jasper said. Then, after a nicely rehearsed pause, 'However, I can sell you a box, which, if you are lucky – and I think you might be – may contain some eggs.'

'How many eggs might be in these boxes?' I asked.

'I have no idea,' he replied. 'Though an educated guess based on the size of the boxes would be that these ones here would likely hold half a dozen, while those ones there would likely contain in the region of twelve.'

'In that case I will have one of your freshest small free-range boxes,' I said.

*

One night, there was a loud bang from the back garden. When I went out to investigate, I found four youths in shell suits standing around a crumpled Fiesta XR3 they had apparently just attempted to park on my next-door neighbour's lawn. Unfortunately for them, a four-foot-high dry stone wall and a large, green, plastic oil tank had intervened. Steam was coming from the bonnet of the vehicle and petrol was trickling across the tarmac.

Seconds after I arrived on the scene, my neighbour Ossie hove into view. Ossie is a big man, a former Royal Marine and rugby forward. He is getting on in years, but though what must once have been an impressive barrel-chest has now relocated southwards, he is still a fearsome sight in his singlet. His local reputation suggested that, in this case, appearances were not deceptive. Ossie was, as the local expression had it, 'a right rough punter'.

Closely following behind Ossie was his wife Nora. 'Go with him Harry,' Nora said in a stage whisper. 'Keep an eye on him and stop him doing anything he'll regret.' I told her I would though, looking at the vast muscles on Ossie's shoulders, his balled fists and the grim set of his jaw, I wasn't sure quite how I'd go about it. I imagined my best chance would be to shriek and fall to the floor feigning some kind of fit.

As Ossie strode towards the youths, one of them, a spotty lad sporting a Burberry baseball cap and a vivid necklace of lovebites, attempted diplomacy: 'I suppose the main thing,' he said nervously, eyeing the veins which were by this point bulging like strands of blue spaghetti amidst the rich passata of my neighbour's face, 'is that nobody was hurt.' Ossie is a retired police sergeant. Twenty-five years' patrolling rough pit-villages in the foothills of the north Pennines have left him with a firm belief in the educative properties of pain.

'I dunno,' he snarled at the lad. 'If you'd have broke your effing legs it might've taught you something.'

Made nervous by this outburst one of the lads attempted to light a cigarette. 'Oh, that's right,' Ossie boomed. 'Blow us all up now, you bloody moron.'

'Steady on, mate,' the largest of the lads said.

Ossie glared at him. 'Open your mouth again and I'll hoy you in the river,' he snarled. 'And I'll tell you what, you'll find it effing hard to get out with both your arms fractured.' There was no further repartee and a police van arrived soon afterwards.

The next day, when I took Manny out, I met an old lady from the village. 'Someone's been doing some landscaping on Ossie's garden, I see,' she said. 'Driver about eighteen, black hair, walks like he's got a coconut under each arm?' I said that would be about right. 'Oh aye,' the old lady said sagely. 'We minded it would be that Dowling lad.'

Later on my walk I bumped into Tommy. 'Made a bit of a mess of Ossie's wall, haven't they? Dowling, was it?'

When I met Mr Dodds he shook his head. 'I hear you've had a bit of a drama,' he said. 'I reckon that Dowling would have been there or thereabouts.'

Impressive though it may have sounded, this was hardly Miss Marple-style deduction. In every village there is always one criminal family. And everyone, including the coppers, knows who they are. It should be pointed out that these people are not exactly the Krays, their activities have no patina of spurious glamour. They do not sport sharp designer suits, Italian sunglasses or engage in high-level corporate crime. If they are involved in money laundering it is only because they have forgotten to check the pockets of their trousers when they bung them in the washing machine.

The criminal family in the village where I grew up were the Barlows. The eldest son Kevin Barlow, having built up a fearsome fighting reputation behind various bike sheds and scout huts, foolishly took to boxing. When I was eight he was selected for the England schoolboy team for an international with Scotland and we all went to see him. The venue was the assembly hall of a Teesside school. The fighters walked to the ring down a corridor plastered with French verb conjugations and posters charting the journey of the cocoa bean from West Africa to the corner shop.

Unlike most professional boxers, Kevin Barlow did not have a ring nickname but the prevailing view in our village was that, if he had, the ring announcer would have introduced him as Kevin 'A thoroughly bad lot Barlow' Barlow. We all thought of Kevin Barlow as a dangerous reprobate. Unfortunately, on the night in question he found himself in the ring with a boy from Glasgow. I have no wish to engage in regional stereotyping here, but I think it is fair to say that in a fight between the hardest boy in Glasgow and the hardest boy from a North Riding village there will generally only be one winner. Kevin Barlow took a right pasting. By the end of the first round his face seemed to be pointing in several different directions at the same time. He was knocked out in round two.

Kevin's younger brother Carl was in my class. He was a bumbling lad with a head like an old and roughly used turnip. One Sunday night, when he was sixteen, Carl committed an act that exemplifies rural crime in all its desperate dumbness. He broke into the village barber's shop. The barber was an old-fashioned sort with a belief in the beauty of the unadorned masculine skull. He even regarded ears as an over-elaboration, or that at least is what you might have thought from the number of times he nicked them with his clippers. In keeping with the barber's ascetic approach to haircare, there was nothing on his premises but ample quantities of those twin mainstays of the traditional male grooming salon: tubs of white grease and boxes of prophylactics. Naturally enough, following the break-in Carl was swiftly apprehended, the police having adopted the simple expedient of calling at the Barlow house the minute they heard a burglary had occurred. He was found guilty and sent to Borstal.

Years later, the crime came up in conversation in the local pub. 'Never understood why he did it,' someone said. 'There was nowt in there but Brylcreem and Durex.' 'Aye,' came the reply. 'But who knows, mebbe Carl was planning on running away to Paris and setting himself up as a gigolo.'

The sheep had been put out in the church field so I had to keep a careful hold on Manny. Like Ingo before him he would happily have pursued the flock. I doubted that Manny would have actually bitten any of them, but violence was hardly necessary to do damage to a sheep. When people talked about a dog 'worrying' a sheep I often thought they meant it literally. If you burst a paper bag behind a sheep it would likely keel over.

If the sheep had had the sense to stand their ground there would have been no problem. Farm cats knew better than to scarper when a dog ran towards them. They stood their ground until it was a few yards away and then did that electric shock thing with their fur and hissed. Even fierce dogs were frightened by that. Ossie and Nora had an old farm cat named Penny. The first time Ingemar saw her he charged instantly. Penny fizzed and spat. Ingo put the brakes on and yodelled pitifully by way of apology. The two of them soon came to an understanding. On warm days they'd enjoy the fresh air together in the garden, Penny lying on the garden bench and Ingemar lying under it.

Sheep, though, had never learned. Or rather they had unlearned what they had once known. Robert Bakewell was one of the founders of modern agriculture. At his farm at Dishley in Leicestershire during the middle years of the eighteenth century, Bakewell used a strict selective breeding policy to improve the size, fecundity and growth speed of his livestock, though perhaps selective inbreeding might be a more accurate term, since the methods employed often involved the mating of closely related animals. In a dispute that in many ways mirrors the current arguments over genetic engineering, many people expressed fears about what Bakewell was doing, citing biblical injunctions against incest and predicting deformity and chaos.

One of the new breeds Bakewell produced by his techniques was the New Leicester sheep, a big, fast-maturing animal that was so coveted by other farmers he was able to hire out his prize ram, Two Pounder, for a mighty 1200 guineas per season. A contemporary painting exists of Two Pounder. It depicts him as barrel-shaped, with such short legs that his most valuable assets are practically bumping along the ground. He appears to be wearing a sly grin. Perhaps that is not so surprising. After all the only other creature to have been paid so much money to have sex was Demi Moore in *Indecent Proposal*.

Spiritually, if not quite literally, Two Pounder was the father of many of today's sheep breeds. One of those directly descended from him is the Bluefaced Leicester. The Bluefaced Leicester is a large, baggy beast with a pronounced roman nose and a lugubrious mien that seems to express a lifetime of disappointment. Those who tend our nation's flocks and herds are rightly wary of the sentimental imaginings of outsiders when it comes to animals, but I think that to suggest that this is a very depressed sheep is more than simply anthropomorphism.

Mr Dodds had spent fifty years of his life as a hill farmer. It had left him with a face imbued with all the weatherbeaten stoicism of a tree-stump. The only thing I have ever known to crack his mask were the words 'Bluefaced Leicester'. On hearing them, his mouth curled and his eyes narrowed until he wore the expression of a man who has just discovered why you should never walk through a field of cows wearing flip-flops. 'The Bluefaced Leicester,' he snarled vehemently, 'has only one ambition in life and that is to die. The slightest breath of wind and she'll up and fall over. The hardest work man ever set himself was saving that blasted animal from extinction.'

Sadly the Bluefaced Leicester is not the only sheep with a death wish. I once asked a friend who farms in the North York Moors how he located his flock in heavy snow. 'When looking for sheep,' he said, 'the first thing to do is to ask yourself the question: where would I go if I was trapped in this blizzard? The leeward side of a wall would be the obvious place. And once you've identified the spot that an animal with even the slightest survival instinct would head for, then you can eliminate that from your search. Because there is no way that a sheep will have gone there.'

Even the sturdy Herdwick, the grey-fleeced, white-cheeked Lakeland sheep whose fortunes were revived by the intervention of Beatrix Potter, draws a sharp intake of breath and the words, 'By God, but they don't exactly battle to keep themselves alive,' from one man employed to look after them.

Despite these wise and accurate assessments and the kamikaze habit upland sheep have of throwing themselves in front of passing vehicles, it would be wrong to think that our flocks are actively suicidal. It is more that any zest for life they once possessed has been bred out of them.

The wild sheep, such as the European mouflon, are tough, resourceful and courageous enough to keep a wolf at bay. Most of his domesticated kin have not the sense to scrape away the snow with their hooves to find the grass beneath. Dogs, cats, goats and horses can all fend for themselves, if necessary, but there is no such thing as a feral ewe. No animal has lost more during the process of domestication than the sheep. Bakewell's opponents worried that he would create a monster. Instead he created a hapless, nervous ninny.

In the pet shop they had dog chews made from cowhide that were shaped like little baby bootees. 'Made in Thailand' it said on the label. I thought of the workers making them out there in Siam. They must have thought that western babies were being made to wear very hard footwear. 'Won't these hurt the children's feet?' they would ask their boss. And the boss would shake his head, smile and say, 'Ah no, these are not for children. They are for the dogs.' And the Thai workers would imagine the westerners bending down and tying the laces on their pets' shoes and wonder just how rich and crazy we must be.

They'd have pondered even harder if they'd seen the mail-order catalogue of dog gifts my mum had got from a very smart American outfitter especially for Little Man. The catalogue had all sorts of things in it designed to pep up your pet's life. There was, for example, a ramp that slid down from the boot of an estate car so that the dog was saved the exertion of having to actually jump into it. There were dog safety belts, a variety of feather beds, glove puppets (presumably for you to entertain the dog with rather than vice versa), dog hot water bottles and pet coats, both waterproof and fleecy. 'Strange there isn't a dog hot tub,' I said when I looked at it.

'Or a dog chocolate fountain,' Maisie added.

My mother bought Manny two toys from the catalogue for his birthday – a fluffy cockerel and a large woolly mammoth that squawked when you squeezed it. Both seemed fairly comical until you saw a dog with them in its mouth. When Manny picked it up, the cockerel's head and wing flopped realistically to one side, the mammoth meanwhile looked uncannily like a dead hare. It was clear they had been rather skilfully designed to provide accuracy without controversy.

Manny liked the toys a lot, especially the cockerel. He'd run the full length of the house at top speed with it in his jaws, drop it by the cast-iron wood burner in the kitchen, run around the table and grab it again, then he'd hurtle back down the house, toss the chicken in the air so it landed behind him, spin round and pounce on it. He could carry on with the game for a quarter of an hour. When he was tired he'd take the chicken up on to a low day-bed in the sitting room. He'd place it right on the edge, lie down and gently nudge it with his nose. When it wobbled and began to fall he'd leap forward and try to catch it before it hit the ground.

Watching Manny playing like this was proof that dogs can think imaginatively, that they can pretend. In the past, whenever I'd watched any of our dogs sitting quietly, staring into space, I'd thought of the old joke about the night watchman and what he did during his long and lonely shift: 'Sometimes I sits and thinks, but mainly I just sits.' Now I wasn't so sure. If dogs could invent make-believe games, maybe they could daydream too. Perhaps when Manny lay blinking on the mat by the radiator in my office he was secretly active in a fantasy world, swinging through the jungles of Africa, or saving the planet from evil super-villains.

Manny was particularly gentle with his toys. The day after he arrived, Maisie had given him one of her massive collection of Beanie Babies (if you need any loft insulation please get in touch), a little brown bear. Two years later it was still in one piece. If she'd given it to Ingemar it wouldn't have lasted past teatime.

When Ingo was given a toy he would lie down with it between his paws and systematically destroy it, nipping a little bit off at a time and spitting it on to the floor. Once my mother had given him a big squeaky rubber bone for Christmas. It had taken him less than ten minutes to reduce it to a pile of confetti-sized pieces after which he had got up, sighed and wandered off to his bed. 'Well, he didn't reckon much to that, did he?' my dad said.

Later, when my mother was picking up the debris she said, 'That's funny. I can't find the squeak. D'you think Ingo swallowed it?'

'We'll find out when he farts,' my dad remarked, blowing a high-pitched raspberry.

Manny and Ingo were very different characters. Since one breed was French and the other German it was hard not to see this difference in terms of nationality. Manny was full of elan. He was small, cheeky and mercurial. Ingo, by contrast, was big, solid and serious. He was not given to complaining. Once when I was out in the garden talking to Ossie, Ingo had sat right beside me for the whole half-hour conversation. It was only when I went to go in that I noticed the reason that he had stayed so close. It wasn't loyalty – I was standing on his paw.

While PBGV's characteristic call was his cheery cry of 'Arrrrroooo!', the schnauzer's most famous vocal characteristic was its deep, regretful sigh. When Ingo was offered a biscuit he sat to attention looking straight up at you, the only sign of his excitement the almost imperceptible shifting of his weight from one front paw to the other. Looking down at him, the close cropped head, serious eyes and drooping moustaches, I was put in mind of a Potsdam grenadier receiving a commendation from Frederick the Great.

When Manny was in trouble his reaction was to launch a charm offensive, scampering around the house, throwing his toys in the air, in an attempt to make you laugh. When Ingo was told off he harrumphed mournfully and slouched away like a gentleman who had brought dishonour on the family name. When he had done something really naughty – like the time we left him in the car with the shopping and he rooted through two carrier bags until he found a large carrot cake, which he then proceeded to eat, paper bag, cling-film wrap and all – he would take it so much to heart I often thought that if he could have found a revolver he'd have retired to his study and done the decent thing.

When Manny was at his food dish and he bent to eat the ring on his collar banged against the ceramic bowl just before his jaws reached the biscuits. He ate in staccato gulps pausing after every second one to swallow. Ting-ting, chomp-chomp. Ting-ting, chomp-chomp. Compared to Ingo, he ate extremely daintily. Sometimes we'd listen to him eating for five minutes or more and yet when he stepped away from his dish it was still half full. Ingo wolfed the whole lot in less than a minute and then ran off to wipe his meaty beard on the bottom of the sitting room curtains. I liked to think that this reflected their respective national attitudes to gastronomy. 'Manny believes in taking time over his repast,' I said. 'You know, in France lunch can last for several hours.'

I snuck out of the house slightly early that lunchtime. It was Sunday and I'd heard a rumour that there were Jehovah's Witnesses around. Whenever I saw a Jehovah's Witness I thought of my grandfather. One Sunday morning, when I was a child and was staying at my grandparents' house in Marske, there'd been a knock at the door and my granddad, who was still in his vest – it being his habit never to put a shirt on until after he'd shaved – went and opened it. Standing on the doorstep were two men, soberly dressed in dark suits. One of the men was considerably older than the other. 'Thousands live that never die,' he announced. My granddad looked at him. 'The poor buggers,' he said, shut the door in the men's faces and went back to reading the *Sunday Post*. He never commented on the incident again.

I moved silently along the hedge down the main road, side-stepping a couple of joggers, who offered a breathy, 'Thanks,' and carried on their way. Walkers are expected to give way to joggers. I am never quite sure why. Half the time the walkers are the ones travelling the fastest. In fact, some joggers move so slowly I'm never sure if they'd make more rapid progress by just running on the spot and letting the spinning of the earth do the work for them. After the joggers, I slid stealthily along the hedge until I reached the cut down to the river.

Down on the bank I relaxed a bit. A kingfisher flashed past, a streak of improbably vivid blue whizzing, missile-like, over the dark water and disappearing in the direction of Carlisle. Even before the inhabitants of these islands knew that South America or Africa existed, they must have sensed that somewhere there was a place more vibrant and exotic from seeing the kingfisher. It was a bird so bright that every time you saw one it was like a sneak preview of the tropics.

I let Manny off when we got to the big field. He was relatively safe in here. It was well fenced and no deer came through it. There were plenty of rabbits, though, and he'd soon disappeared into a low thicket of broom, gorse and birch saplings. Every once in a while I'd catch sight of him. Or rather, I'd catch sight of part of him.

According to the breed books the petit basset griffon Vendéen carried its tail 'like a sabre'. This sounded very dashing and was, for the most part, apt, though I suspect that if any fencing coach had seen a pupil waving his sword around quite so crazily he'd have slapped him round the ear. The PBGV's tail is one of its many fine features. It is a very active tail. When Manny is pleased or excited, or when he is tucking into his dinner it quivers like a dowsing rod. The Vendéen's tail is more than just decorative. It also serves a useful purpose. When Little Man is trailing rabbits in the undergrowth by the river, quite often the only bit of him I can see is his vigorously vibrating tail. It's like a signal flag.

After five minutes of watching the occasional flash of his tail I blew on my dog whistle. It was an Acme 3.5. I wasn't sure how the 3 and the 4 differed from it. The 3.5 made an impressively loud and shrill peep. The first time I used it my ears popped. Manny didn't exactly come to it when I blew it – he was far too busy. But at least when I blew it he knew where I was when he finally got bored, or decided he wanted his tea.

As I watched Manny, Mr Fudgie came along with Fudge. Mr Fudgie said the dog was well but he himself was feeling a little sheepish. Mr Fudgie was a notorious practical joker. He was always pulling elaborate pranks on friends and workmates, disguising himself as a flood defence officer, or phoning up pretending to be from the football pools. The previous evening, however, he had pulled a stunt that had gone awry.

Mr Fudgie's wife had gone shopping at the Metro Centre. She phoned him and asked would he meet her off the train at 6.30. Mr Fudgie went down to the station. He got there ten minutes early and while he was sitting in the car a sudden inspiration came over him: he'd go to the platform, hide in one of the big salt bins they have there and when Mrs Fudgie came past he'd jump out and give her a big fright. He considered this would be a right laugh and so he went and hid in the salt bin, raising the lid just the slightest amount so that he had a slit of visibility. The train arrived and sure enough Mr Fudgie saw the legs of a woman flanked by several shopping bags approaching. When they came opposite he flung open the lid of the salt bin and leapt up yelling, 'Aaaaaaargh!'

The woman shrieked in terror and hurled her shopping

bags thirty feet in the air. She was a total stranger. 'Oh hell,' Mr Fudgie said. 'I'm really sorry, love, I thought you were the missus.' And with that explanation he wandered off back to his car to check his mobile. Mrs Fudgie had left a message to say she'd missed the train and would be on the next one instead. 'I decided that, on balance, it was probably best not to hide in the salt bin again,' Mr Fudgie said.

June

We moved up to Northumberland from the Old Kent Road in London. It was June. The removal men had driven down from Newcastle, picked up our stuff and driven back again. The following day they brought our belongings out to the village. 'Hey, bit different, this, from what you're used to,' one of the removal men said. That was certainly true.

The Old Kent Road was a place of notorious and traditional violence. Fights in the local pubs spilled out across the pavement and stopped the traffic. The arrival of the police tended only to make things worse. There was an historical antipathy towards the police in the area that went back to the days when it was the home turf of the costermongers – a group who felt that the constabulary victimised them. An officer interviewed on a local crime watch programme told how he and his colleagues entered a pub to the invariable greeting of a shower of bottles and glasses. 'The worst thing about it,' he said, with an admirable sense of chivalry, 'is that a lot of those doing the throwing are women.'

When I told Tommy where we'd come from he pulled a face. 'I knew this Cockney lad when I did my national service. He came from the Old Kent Road,' Tommy said. 'We were out at Hamlin in Germany and he spent the whole time having a go about how primitive the north of England was: coal in the bath – you know the crack. "When we gets demobbed, Tom," he used to say, "you come down the Smoke an' stay with me. See a bit of civilisation." So I did.'

'He lived down by that boxing pub, the Thomas à Becket. I got round to his house about three in the afternoon. My mate answers the door and takes me through into the scullery. His dad and three of his cronies are sat at the table in their vests playing cribbage. His dad says, "Alright, Tom? Make yourself at home, son. Take your shirt off."

'That night we went out for a drink. This is 1951. The Old Kent Road was heaving. People were flying out of pub doorways. One bloke came out through the plate glass window of a bar and went straight back in to collect his cap. It was like the ruddy Wild West.'

I told him that, while the rest of Britain had changed, the Old Kent Road had retained its old-world charms. Tommy grimaced. 'I bet these two fellas wouldn't like it down there,' he said, indicating the dogs.

I said I thought not. The only dogs you saw in the Old Kent Road were huge and fierce. The man who lived in the flat downstairs from us had a bull terrier with one dark eye and one red eye. It looked like a gang leader out of *Escape From New York*. The man who owned the bull terrier was large and middle-aged. He had a vast and bulky torso, but his fat was solid rather than flabby. It was the sort of weight you throw around. He dressed in pastel-coloured polo shirts, bleached, pressed jeans and tassel loafers. He drove a Mercedes with a personalised number-plate. I can't remember what it was, but in my mind I see 'GBH 1'. I never found out what he did for a living, though I am willing to bet he wasn't a window dresser.

Despite that, I should add that at times the Old Kent Road was strangely whimsical. The landlord of the pub opposite our flat, for instance, had AstroTurfed the flat roof of his premises, built a patio wall round the parapet, arranged white garden furniture within and erected a small garden shed in one corner. On hot afternoons he appeared on the roof in Bermuda shorts and Ray-Bans and reclined on a sun-lounger, sipping from a glass of white wine, while twelve feet below six lanes of traffic rumbled by on the main London-to-Dover road.

One warm afternoon I stood with an old schoolmate of mine who farms in one of the skiff-shaped valleys that run into Eskdale. In common with most people from the North Riding, his delivery is so deadpan he makes Buster Keaton look like Jim Carrey. 'See that road?' he asked, pointing across the dale. The road ran diagonally down the steep hillside, whose merging summer colours gave it the appearance of a rather snappy tweed. Near the bottom it was engulfed by hedgerows spattered with foamy white elderflower and creamy cow parsley. 'I was stood out here one day and a couple of cyclists come down there,' he continued. 'They were talking to one another and I could hear every word clear as a bell. I thought to myself: I bet there's not many places in England so quiet that you can listen in on a conversation that's going on over a mile away. It's a really marvellous place is this,' he paused for a moment to let the thought sink in. 'And then, of course, it pissed down,' he said.

We were in a field down from his house watching his dogs round up sheep. Manny was in the car. Manny chased sheep. Every dog I or my family has ever owned has chased sheep, all except one, a slight and sickly Westie called Mac, who was too nervous even to chase his own tail. In fact, it was probably fear that his tail was about to chase him that made Mac so neurotic. Sometimes I watched Mac, with his skinny legs, fine fur and the distinctly un-terrier-like tentativeness of his movements, and I couldn't help wondering if there wasn't a bit of Siamese cat somewhere in his gene pool. Poor Mac. It wasn't his fault. He'd had a deprived puppyhood. My mother had wanted a second West Highland to keep Doogie company while she was out at work. Somebody told her they knew a woman in a nearby village whose son had some Westie pups for sale. So we rang him and went over to see them. There were four in a cardboard box in a shed. The mother was nowhere in evidence. 'Where are these from?' my mother asked the young man.

'Oh, from Scotland,' he said quickly. There was something shifty and nervous about him.

'I'll take one of the dogs,' my mother said. The young man wanted cash, so we had to go off to the bank to get it. 'Those poor things are from a puppy farm,' my mother said.

We took Mac away. That night he vomited frothy liquid and his eyes reddened and filled with pus. The next day we took him to the vet. The vet asked where Mac had come from. My mother told him.

'He's only about six weeks old,' the vet said. 'He shouldn't be away from his mother yet. The problem with his eyes is because he's been washed with shampoo. Do you want me to phone the RSPCA?' My mother said she thought that would be a good idea.

When we got home my mother phoned the young man who had sold us Mac. I could hear her voice gradually rising in anger. 'Bring him back?' she snapped towards the end of the conversation. 'You must think I'm completely bloody deranged if you think I'd ever entrust a dog to your care. You're a pathetic little twerp and if I ever see you again, you can rest assured the police will be pulling my fist from up your nose.' My grandfather was sitting in the kitchen eating a pork pie while this was going on. When he heard the last line he smiled quietly to himself. She was his daughter all right. Mac survived and lived to be twelve years old, but he never chased sheep. Doogie did even though they were ten times bigger than him and so did Sam the spaniel even though he couldn't actually see them.

I know plenty of other people with large, bouncy dogs that don't chase sheep, but I have never been so blessed. When we got Ingemar I thought I had at last struck lucky. We used to walk through fields of sheep with him off the lead and he never even looked at them. Once, we picnicked in a meadow filled with lugubrious looking Leicesters. Ingo chased a Frisbee but he never bothered the sheep. That was when he was a pup. Then one day, when he was about nine months old, I let him off in a field of sheep as usual and he looked at them and – pop – a lightbulb clicked on in his head. It was like an adolescent boy suddenly noticing girls for the first time. I had to run 800 yards to catch him. And that was that.

There is a big distinction, of course, between chasing animals and herding them. It was during the height of the Elizabethan wool trade that dogs were first used to

herd sheep in this country. In those days it has been esti-
mated that the ovine population of England exceeded the
human population of today. The vast, heavy-fleeced flocks
were patrolled and cajoled by a breed of dog called the
bobtail, forebears of the Old English sheepdog. Nowadays
you never see an Old English sheepdog working a herd.
There is a good reason for this. And it is not just that the
pay in advertising is better.

One of my friend's Border collies was trying to herd a
trio of Swaledale cross-breeds. The dog was young and
had the over-effusive manner of a package-tour rep. He
was called Jet. All working collies seem to have monosyl-
labic names – Bud, Jess, Fly. Later I asked my friend's
wife if she had ever come across any with longer ones.
'Aye,' she said. 'There was a fella over by Pickering. Very
fond of beer, he was. He got a new dog and called it
Firkin.' There was a pause. 'Well, he did until he'd
shouted, "Firkin, get here!" a few times. I think it's called
Rab now.'

Jet lolloped around the field desperately trying to jolly
the sheep along. While two were content to play along, the
other one just stood and stared at him. The dog backed off
and regrouped. He lowered his body, pulled back his ears
and narrowed his eyes. It was a pose that should have
conjured up images of the hunting wolf, but in Jet's case it
put me more in mind of that chinless young master in the
Molesworth books who tells the rioting boys, 'You may
think I'm soft, but I'm hard, damned hard.'

The recalcitrant sheep didn't buy the new performance
either. She watched Jet advance towards her and then,
when the dog was no more than three yards away, she
dropped her head and began nonchalantly munching the
grass. It was an unmistakable gesture of contempt.

Beside me my friend exhaled loudly, 'Bloody useless,' he hissed. I asked why. 'He's weak and they can sense it,' my friend said. To prove his point he called back Jet and set his older dog, Dan, away. Dan advanced on the rebellious ewe in much the same low-bellied way as Jet. However, it was plain that in his case it was no act. His eyes burned with something ancient and malignant. The sheep took one look at Dan and ran for it.

It was partly because of dogs like Dan that the Old English sheepdog lost its position as a farm worker. Mainly, though, it was because of sheep like the one that had so rudely rebuffed Jet. When the bobtail began its working life most English flocks were made up of large, docile downland sheep. Hardier upland breeds, such as the Swaledales that had thwarted Jet or the ubiquitous Scottish blackface, retain some of the agile, independent attitude of their wild ancestors. The black, four-horned Hebridean sheep, one of the oldest domesticated breeds, is notoriously hard to herd. So much so, in fact, that at one time in the Western Isles dogs were trained not to chivvy the sheep but to chase after them, pull them to the ground and then sit on them until the shepherd arrived and took over. Mind you, the Hebridean sheep had more reason to run than most. Up until the nineteenth century the islands' farmers refused to use shears. Instead, their flocks were plucked.

The collie, originally brought to England by Scottish drovers (the name comes from the Gaelic *cuilean*, 'puppy') had been bred to deal with such sheep. Sometimes it did so so fiercely that early shepherds thought it wise to remove the dogs' canine teeth and subjected the rest to regular filing. These rugged dogs, capable of mastering any flock, quickly superseded the bumbling bobtail. The collie was tough and elemental and remains so to this day. Or, at least, in most cases he does.

When I left my friend's house later that day, Jet was out in the yard. He'd corralled half a dozen bantams into a corner and was watching them diligently. Every time one tried to peel away he cut it off and drove it back to the flock. 'He seems to be able to handle them all right,' I said.

'Oh aye,' my friend replied with a rueful grin. 'Next time I have to bring five hundred chickens down off the moor top for shearing he's going to come in very handy.'

'Not been molested by a panther, then?' Mr Dodds asked when we bumped into him and Taffy on the riverbank near the silver birches. I said I had thus far escaped such a fate. 'It was in the paper again, mind,' Mr Dodds said. I said that wasn't so surprising given that it was summer.

Every year around this time the big cats appeared on the front page of my local paper alongside other matters of rural concern: bypass protests, hospital closures and dogs that have choked to death on cheese. They were as sure a sign of the approach of summer as the twittering of swallows and the roar of Dutchmen's motorcycles, fresh off the boat from IJmuiden.

While the trees are in blossom and the days are long, giant felines roam around this part of Northumberland, strolling in suburban gardens, lolloping along the side of railway lines and harassing sheep and chickens. Once the harvest is home and the weight of berries bows the branches of the elder, however, the panthers mysteriously disappear.

Though no one else seems yet to have made the connection, I cannot help wondering whether the fact that their departure coincides with the ending of the summer ferry service from North Shields to Hamburg is more than simple blind chance. The big cat phenomenon is common to practically every unspoilt area of Britain. Experts who have made a study of British panthers tell us that they stand about two feet high at the shoulder, weigh around seventy pounds, have smooth fur and come in two colours: dull yellow and black. Since this description also fits that of the common Labrador, there are those who are sceptical about the sightings. I fit into this category. Mind you, I am careful to whom I reveal this scepticism. Last year I got into an argument about the existence of the big cats with the builder who was fixing our roof. 'You shouldn't be so cynical,' he said, and somehow I knew what was coming next. For there is an immutable law in these matters which dictates that, at some point, Shakespeare will be quoted. The immortal Bard was a fount of wisdom whose name should be honoured daily, but there is one line for which he deserved belabouring about his shiny pate with a flat-iron. 'After all,' the builder said, 'there are more things in heaven and earth.'

Flush with success, he continued: 'I mean, some people don't believe in mental illness.'

'They would if they listened to you for thirty seconds,' I replied. He still hasn't been back to re-point the chimney.

A belief in no-conclusive-proof theory is the thing that underpins the philosophy of all people who hero-worship *The X-Files*' male protagonist Agent Fox Mulder (catch-phrase: 'There's got be an irrational explanation for this'), a man incapable of misplacing one of his own cufflinks without suspecting alien abduction. That, and a ferocious will to believe. A few years ago, Channel 4 ran an excellent documentary about another British big cat, the infamous Beast of Bodmin. One memorable scene featured two men watching video footage of a small area of Cornish woodland. After many hours, a cat-like creature leapt briefly into shot. After replaying the film over and over again, one of the men sadly conceded that the animal was far too small to be a panther. His colleague was not so easily deterred. 'You're right,' he said excitedly. 'It's obviously a cub.'

Mr Dodds did not believe in British big cats, but Mr Fudgie did. Mr Fudgie said that his son had a friend who was a gamekeeper over near Consett and he had 'seen some pretty odd things early in the morning'. I told Mr Fudgie that if you went to Consett at any time of day you'd be likely to see some pretty odd things, but he was not to be deflected by sarcasm. 'These are countrymen,' he said gravely. 'They know the lie of the land.'

'Yes,' I said, but in the early morning or late at night the light is deceptive. Quite often I think I see somebody standing by the side of the road when I'm out with Manny and then when I get nearer it turns out to be a sign, or a bush I've seen every day for the past ten years. At night the fellow across the road's security lights go on and they shine on a telephone pole in the middle of the field in such a way it looks like it's on fire.'

'Well, I know,' said Mr Fudgie. 'But to be fair neither you or I are country folk. These people are closer to nature. They know what they've seen.'

'My daughter,' I said to Mr Fudgie, 'was in her younger days something of an aficionado of Laura Ingles Wilder. There is a story in *Little House in the Big Woods* concerning Pa Wilder that is pertinent to our current debate. Pa is coming home one winter evening from visiting town. It is late and the light is dim. As he comes around a bend he sees a bear squatting by the side of the track. Pa is shocked and afraid because he doesn't have a gun with him and it is autumn and bears are hungry and crotchety and likely to attack. He knows if he tries to avoid the bear by going into the woods he may get lost in the dark, and if he stays put he will likely freeze to death. So he decides that the only course of action open to him is to try and startle the bear into flight by running straight at it yelling at the top of his lungs. Pa summons up all his courage, takes a deep breath and does just that. The bear doesn't move an inch. Pa gets closer and closer and still the big beast doesn't budge. Pa believes he is entering the last short phase of his life. He thinks he's a goner. He screws up his eyes and bellows even louder and waves his arms and charges on. And suddenly he sees why the bear isn't moving. It isn't a bear at all. It's a tree stump.

'Now,' I said to Mr Fudgie, 'if you know Laura Ingles Wilder you'll know that Pa is an exemplary woodsman, a fine hunter. He is level headed and brave, and he never touches a drop of liquor. And my point is that if Pa can mistake a tree stump for a bear then anybody else could mistake anything for anything.'

'That's as maybe,' Mr Fudgie said, 'But . . .' Once people believe in something like big cats it's really no use arguing with them.

The desire to search out the unknown is really nothing new, of course. It's just that finding anything not already documented becomes harder and harder. I grew up in the North Yorkshire village where Captain James Cook received his schooling. In Cook's day, if you hankered after discovery you got on a ship and went off in search of Australia. Nowadays you have to content yourself with staring out of the kitchen window, camcorder in hand, in the hope that a leopard will jump over the larch-lap fence and clear the occupants of the bird-table away with one snap of its mighty jaws. The natural world has been codified, the globe has been mapped, we live in a time of pygmies. And I should know. Last week I saw a tribe of them behind the local scout hut. They were, in fact, too large to be pygmies. But I reckon they were definitely cubs.

It was early June and the hedgerows were frothing with blossom. Manny stopped to drink from a puddle. It hadn't rained for at least a week and the water was thick and the colour of coffee grounds. Dead flies, diesel oil and plant debris floated on the surface. But Manny lapped happily away at it. Dogs actually prefer dirty water to fresh. I know this for a fact because once, when our family had been for a long walk in the Lake District, Doogie the West Highland proved it beyond doubt. It was a very hot day and when we got back to the car park Doogie was panting. A very nice middle-aged woman was standing leaning on the side of an estate car next to our Austin Maxi. She looked down at Doogie and smiled sympathetically. 'Oh, that poor little fellow looks thirsty,' she said. 'Here, let me give him a drink.' She took a Thermos from the back of the car, poured cold water from it into a Tupperware container and placed it down on the ground in front of our terrier. Doogie sniffed at it suspiciously, then he turned away with a slightly theatrical show of disgust and went off and slurped up from the greenish slime that had gathered in a nearby pothole.

'Honestly, you,' my mother said to Doogie as we drove away. 'You could at least have tried to be polite. That nice lady. I was mortified.'

Catherine, Maisie, Manny and I walked along up an old green lane between high stands of hawthorn and cow parsley. 'Oh, that's Jack-by-the-hedge,' Catherine said whenever Maisie asked her what a white flower was.

'Are you sure?' I invariably replied. 'I think it looks more like lady's smock.'

If I asked Mr Dodds what the same flower was he'd cock his head slightly to one side, squint and say, 'Now, I mind that's old man's beard.' Tommy would likely have scratched his chin and said, 'Well, I don't know what it says in books, but we always call it collier's custards.'

Lord Chesterfield, the eighteenth-century wit and writer, took great exception to the idea that English spelling should be standardised. 'I am a gentleman,' he thundered at the pedants who lined up to scrawl red ink over his manuscripts, 'and I shall spell words how I damn well choose.' I had a good deal of sympathy with his lordship. I also felt his attitude should have been expanded to cover the naming of flowers. At one time every plant had a multitude of names. Then at some point someone had decided what they ought really to be called. Who had done it and under what authority I was never sure.

It was my conviction that beyond the obvious – bluebells, cowslips, primroses, wild violets, wood anemones – most people knew the names of around half a dozen wild flowers and allotted them according to shape and colour. If it was pink and had flat petals I said, 'campion', and Catherine said, 'Actually I think that's ragged robin.' 'Campion is what we called it in North Yorkshire,' I replied.

I felt I was on fairly safe ground playing the regional card. When it came to wild plants the homogenisers had not succeeded quite so well as they had with grammar and punctuation. Things still changed according to where you were. In his book *Food for Free*, Richard Mabey lists

eleven different regional names for wild angelica including
the alarming sounding 'ghost-kex', and close to two dozen
for wood-sorrel ('green sob' was my favourite). Where I
grew up the long sticky weed with the little balls on it that
stick to dogs' fur was called 'grewgrass', Catherine called
it 'goosegrass', but Maisie and her friends called it 'sticky-
jack'.

The only people I've ever met who actually genuinely
did seem to know the proper names of wild flowers were
Catherine's aunts. 'Now that,' they'd say, 'is shepherd's
purse and next to it is tufted vetch. Oh, and look, a little
patch of hare's-foot trefoil surrounding a viper's bugloss.'
The names of the wild flowers were infinitely more elaborate than the plants themselves, most of which were thin
and tiny.

Sometimes even the aunts couldn't identify things. 'I
don't think it's hedge bedstraw,' they'd say. 'The leaves
aren't right, and it's definitely not mouse-ear chickweed,
now I don't suppose it's corn spurrey . . . No it isn't.'

'Well,' I'd say in an attempt to move the debate along,
'my guess would be parson's frottage, but I'm not sure we
get that this far north.'

When I met Mr Dodds near the old green bench he had
Taffy on the lead. 'Don't let your lad come too near him,'
he said. 'There's a bitch in season and it makes him
grumpy.' I looked at Taffy. His ears were back, his shoulders were hunched and his eyes seemed oddly unfocused.
He looked like he was halfway between despair and homi-
cide.

'Oh right,' I said. 'That would explain why this one's
acting so odd.' For two days Manny had been hopping up
and down like a frog in a pump. Every time I got up from

my desk he leapt to his feet. He trailed behind me when I went to put the kettle on, get a biscuit, or pick up the post. When I went in the loo he sat outside the door squeaking. He didn't finish his meals and refused to lie on his bed, preferring instead to adopt the most uncomfortable position he could on the hardest piece of floor in the draughtiest and coldest part of the house. He was terrified of nodding off in case he missed his chance to pounce.

'It'll be that blinking pom-pom pair,' Mr Dodds said. He was a devout Methodist and never swore. Once when we had been walking along together Mr Dodds had tripped on a tree root and exclaimed, 'Ruddy hecking flip!' Listening to him when he was vexed was to be reminded of the kids' comics of yesteryear.

'Have you seen them?' I asked. Mr Dodds shook his head. 'I've seen the blooming car parked, though,' he said.

The 'pom-pom pair' were two blonde Pomeranians named Heidi and Mitzi. They lived in a village about ten miles away. The owners, a retired couple, only brought them to walk in our village when one of the pom-poms was on heat. They came in an unmistakable electric-blue Japanese sports coupé. Whenever I saw it pulled up in the lay-by at the top of the wood my heart sank.

'We bring Mitzi and Heidi here because when they're on heat it drives the dogs at home mad,' one of the owners, a rangy fellow with a lolloping stride, straw-coloured corduroys and a scent of mints and tobacco, had explained to me one day. 'It's a total nuisance.' It drove the dogs in our village mad too but, of course, they weren't likely to follow the Pomeranians home and stand outside their house howling all night.

Like all Pomeranians, Heidi and Mitzi were little and fluffy and dainty, with kittenish faces. They were also the

most unreconstructedly feminine dogs I have ever encountered. They had to be walked on the road because they
didn't like to get their feet dirty, lifted into the car because
they couldn't jump. If a male dog came within ten yards
of them they hid behind their owner's legs whimpering
piteously: 'Oh, do make the brute go away. He is rough
and malodorous and frightens us so.' It was easy to imagine Heidi and Mitzi lounging about the house in feather
mules, eating cocktail snacks, drinking sweet sherry and
reading Mills & Boon romances in between manicures. I
found them profoundly irritating. It was a mystery to me
what Taffy, Manny and the other village dogs saw in them.
It was like a friend admitting to a crush on Dame Barbara
Cartland.

On the topic of the sex lives of dogs my mother often
quoted a dog expert she had seen on television in the
1960s: 'A bitch is on heat twice a year. It lasts for ten days.
A dog is in season just once a year. It lasts for twelve
months.' That seemed about right. Certainly there was
nothing more pitiful than a lovelorn dog. They were
beside themselves, unable to settle, edgy, twitchy, obsessed
to the point of lunacy.

Once, when Ingemar, in thrall to the mysterious allure
of Heidi or Mitzi, had lain by the front door moaning and
sighing all evening, and I had snapped at him several times
to get a grip on himself and shut up so I could watch the
football, Catherine had looked at him and said, 'Poor
thing. Imagine what it's like to be in such a pathetic state.'
I told her I didn't need to imagine – I had once been a
teenaged boy.

Tadger, at least, was not affected by the pom-poms.
This was because he had, as Tommy delicately put it, 'had
his pockets picked'. Tadger had once been quite a Romeo

and several times had disappeared for days on end in pursuit of love. 'The last time, we got a call from a bloke over near Prudhoe.' Tadge had been camped out on his doorstep for two days in the hope of getting trapped off with the other resident, a beautiful Alsatian. 'I had to drive over and pick him up,' Tommy said. 'It must be fifteen miles. And the bitch was about three foot taller than him. I don't know how he was planning to go about it. He'd have needed scaffolding.'

After that, Tommy took Tadger to the vet and had him neutered. 'It doesn't seem to have bothered him that much, really,' Tommy said. 'Though you have to watch him with food. They tend to eat too much and get fat after they've been done.'

I'd heard that before about castrated dogs, that they turned greedy and put on the pounds. 'Did the vet say why that is?' I asked him.

Tommy shook his head, 'Nothing to keep themselves in shape for any more, I suppose,' he said.

July

Little Man and I walked up the back lane that led up to the reservoir path. A retired couple from down the road were out picking litter. It was their hobby. They picked litter all over: a different stretch of road every day. Sometimes when I went out with Manny at 6 a.m. they'd already filled a bin bag with cigarette packets and chip wrappers. When they saw me they lifted their litter-picking sticks in salute, pulling the triggers so that the automated pincers waggled in and out like waving fingers.

By Jasper the binman's cottage there was a row of stiff-looking rabbits lying out on the wall by the chicken coups. 'I've been out netting,' he said.

'You've got ferrets then,' I said.

'Oh, aye. I've got two pair. Do you want to see them?'

I politely refused his kind offer. I had seen one ferret already in my life, and that was enough.

Ferrets were first brought in to the home by the ancient Egyptians as a means of rodent control, their status as a household pet predating that of the cat. In Renaissance Europe the sharp-toothed little animal was regarded as something of a fashion accessory.

Leonardo Da Vinci painted Cecilia Gallerani fondling

a white ferret, while a similar, if smaller, specimen is seen crawling up Elizabeth I's dress in the famous *Ermine Portrait*, which hangs in the Courtauld Gallery.

Later the ferret started to keep company that was rather more suited to its Latin name, 'the little furry thief', turning up amongst the Wild Wooders in *The Wind in the Willows*, as companion to the archetypal 'smelly Herbert' Compo in *Last of the Summer Wine*, and dangling by its incisors from the fingers of TV presenter Richard Whiteley in a famous clip from a local news programme that turns up – alongside the *Blue Peter* pooping elephant – whenever British television viewers are asked to select their best ever TV blooper.

The only ferret I had ever known belonged firmly in this less reputable category. He was an albino male or hob (female ferrets are jills; the young, kits) owned by a schoolfriend of mine and known as Bites-Yer-Legs Norman. Bites-Yer-Legs was named in honour of Leeds United's robustly uncompromising defender, Norman Hunter, but in terms of pure psychotic violence far surpassed even the Yorkshire club's legendary number six.

Bites-Yer-Legs was in a permanent radge. This was because he was a sensitive soul and driven to anger by many things. In fact, it is hard to think of anything that didn't test his patience to breaking point. Even a glimpse of Fonzie on *Happy Days* was likely to end with him sinking his fangs into the nearest Achilles tendon. What really got Norman's goat, though, was flapping material. During the mid seventies it seemed this Yorkshire ferret was the only creature on earth who was actively campaigning for the return of straight-leg jeans.

And then there was the smell. The ferret's closest wild relative is the polecat. The old English name for polecat is foul marten. Ferrets secrete a pungent odour from their anal glands when they are frightened or aggressive. Since Norman spent nearly all his waking hours in a state of extreme belligerence, this meant he lived most of his life enveloped in a poisonous mist. In an enclosed space the stink was so palpable you instinctively swatted at it, as at a cloud of midges.

It is said that Britain and the US are countries separated by a common language. It might also be said that the two nations are divided by a common animal, the ferret, or at least by their attitudes to the only domesticated member of the weasel family.

It is hard to imagine anybody in Britain looking upon a member of the same species as Bites-Yer-Legs Norman as cute or adorable, or feeling the overwhelming urge to pamper it with presents. But such is the case in the US, where ferrets are regarded as just the sweetest little things.

Shops such as The Ferret Store offer the transatlantic ferret-owner the opportunity to purchase all kinds of gifts, from a plush hammock known as 'The Marshall Designer Fleece Leisure Lounge', to an extensive range of deodorant sprays. There even exists a range of ferret-sized hats, including a little straw Stetson.

There is a darker side to the US ferret scene. Sadly, while their fellow American ferrets cavort around in a Sheppard & Greene Ferret Freeway ('Can This Be The Ferret Toy Of The Century?'), others live as fugitives from justice. It is entirely illegal to own a ferret in the state of California. An organisation called Californians for Ferret Legalization (CFL) has been campaigning vigorously to have the ban lifted. According to CFL, there could be as many as 500,000 ferrets living underground, as it were, in the Sunshine State.

Twelve months ago, another group of Californian ferret fans, Ferrets Anonymous, held a rally in San Diego. Fifty of them marched through a local park, defiantly displaying their pets. Sadly, the day ended in tragedy for one outlaw ferret, Rocky, who took exception to media intrusion and bit a cameraman. Rocky was immediately seized by law officers and terminated by lethal injection. 'California Executes Freedom-March Ferret' read the headline on the *Independent Ferret News Service* website.

Some readers may find it ironic that, in a country where you can walk into a shop and buy a Smith & Wesson magnum, it is against the law to own a polecat. But then you never knew Bites-Yer-Legs Norman.

Manny was barking and yelping when we met Mr Dodds by a patch of Himalayan balsam that had been gradually expanding year by year until it now stretched for several hundred yards along the north bank of the river. People had told me that dogs had been poisoned by the pollen of this invading plant, but if that was the case Manny was clearly immune to it.

The reason Manny was so excited was because he had seen a cat. It was the same cat we saw at least once a week and which had that annoying cat habit of not actually running away until it was really, really sure that the thing it was running away from had got a good sight of it. A combination of personal prejudice and close observation had led me long ago to the conclusion that cats enjoyed taunting dogs. Sam, the blind cocker spaniel, had suffered particularly. At least twice a year a cat that lived in the sawmill downstream from our cottage would appear at the top end of the garden and promenade up and down until Sam got wind of it. He would then hurtle

after the cat and the cat would nip off round the corner
and under the neighbour's potting shed. The neighbour's
potting shed was raised on bricks. There was just enough
room under it for a cat to crouch; a dog that wanted to get
under it had to crawl on its belly. Sam would chase the cat
until it ducked in under the shed and hurl himself in after
it. The cat turned around and unsheathed its claws. At
this point a signal would flash through Sam's brain.
Wedged between the ground and the bottom of the shed
he'd frantically attempt to retreat. We'd see his back legs
scrabbling on the soil and then there'd be a terrible yelping and the spaniel would pop out from under the shed
and scamper back to us, his nose a tattered and bloody
mess. And six months later, when the cuts had healed and
the memory of his pain had faded the cat would appear
at the top of the garden and the whole scene would be
replayed.

Mr Dodds didn't like cats either. He said he thought
they were deceptive and devious. 'You always feel they're
looking at you and thinking, "What a blooming idiot!"' He
said. 'People say they're clean because they bury their
mess,' Mr Dodds said. 'But the only reason they do that is
so some poor beggar will stick his fingers in it when he's
planting crocus bulbs. And if I'm sat in a room and there's
six other people who love cats and a cat walks in, guess
who it will make a bee-line for and jump on his knee?
And if you try and shoo it off it sticks its claws into your
leg. If a dog did that you'd clip its ear. Do you ever see a
cat owner cuff their cat? Of course you don't, because
they've got the same superior attitude as their ruddy pets.
If your dog jumped over a cat owner's garden wall, dug a
hole in the best flower bed and did a turnout in it, they'd
be telling you to send it to dog training classes. But when

a cat does the same thing in your garden they just smirk.
They're blinking unhygienic, cats.'

Mr Dodds had formed this latter opinion after an incident in Gateshead back in the 1930s. Mr Dodds had taken
some cattle over to the mart there. 'We went to that mart
about once a month,' he said. 'It had quite big day-sales
and lots of farmers came from across Durham and
Northumberland and after the sale we all went into the
big canteen there and had a mug of tea, a scone and a bit
of craic.'

Mr Dodds said that when you went into the canteen,
after the sale had finished, the scones were all lined up,
one per plate, buttered. 'And they weren't mean with it,'
Mr Dodds said. 'When you bit into one of them scones
you could see your teeth in that butter.' Mr Dodds said
that he and his father always had one of the scones and so
did most of the other farmers they knew. They must have
sold about a hundred every mart day, he said.

On this particular day, Mr Dodds had taken the cattle
to market on his own. His father had had to stay at the
farm because someone from the brewery was coming out
to inspect his barley and see if it was brewing grade. 'If
your barley was good enough for brewing it was a big
deal,' he said, 'because you got about double the price for
it.' He said he'd phone his father when the cattle were sold
and let him know what they had gone for. Mr Dodds'
cattle were sold mid morning and he asked a steward
where the nearest payphone was and the steward said
there was one in the canteen.

'So I went into the canteen,' Mr Dodds said, 'and there
was nobody else there, but all the buttered scones were out
on the plates in neat rows. I went over to the phone and
spoke to my father and as I was talking to him I noticed

this big, fat tortoiseshell cat appear at a window over by the tea urns. The window was propped open to let out the steam and this cat pushed its way through the gap and on to the sill. It sprang down on to the work surface and it walked very slowly past the tea urns and on to the table with the scones on it. And then, this blinking cat promenaded ever so deliberately down those rows of scones and he licked,' here Mr Dodds flicked out his tongue, 'the butter on every single ruddy one of them. And when he had done that he sort of sauntered back with this smug look on his face, jumped on to the window ledge and disappeared out of the window.'

Mr Dodds shook his head, 'I bet he'd done that every flipping time the mart was on. I'd eaten dozens of those scones. And that,' he said, 'is why I don't like cats.'

Our daughter Maisie was born in July. Giving birth is apparently highly painful. For the father, though, the most grisly and gruesome moments come before the birth when young mothers come to visit and pass on their congratulations. This is when the childbirth stories start. They are so horrible, so filled with blood and agony they make *Reservoir Dogs* look like *Pollyanna*. Even a man such as myself, raised on the card-playing gamesmanship of Mrs Metcalfe, struggled to cope.

When it comes to childbirth stories it seems there is always somebody worse off, and that somebody is the person sitting next to the woman who is currently telling her childbirth story. It is like a masochistic version of Monty Python's 'Four Yorkshiremen' sketch. The scene begins when the first-time mother-to-be tentatively asks if labour hurts. After much laughter, thigh-slapping and general hullabaloo young mother number one will say, 'I was in labour for ten hours and the pain was so intense I grabbed my husband's wrist and squeezed so hard his fingers turned blue.'

After a pause young mother number two takes a deep breath and commences, 'My labour went on for eighteen hours, and the pain? I yelled so loud my Bob still has ringing in his ears to this day.' The third woman then sits forward in her chair and says, 'Twenty-four hours. Husband's arm wrenched clean off at the shoulder.'

And then they will all sit back and smile and say, 'Ee, yes, it's the most wonderful gift that nature can bestow. I envy you pet, I really do.' And they're not being sarcastic either. When you have survived dozens of childbirth stories the actual birth is a doddle.

When we brought Maisie home from the maternity ward, Ingo – who was aged five at the time – accepted the new situation with surprising equanimity. The crying, the commotion, the fact that visitors who had once fussed over him now strode past without a second glance in his direction – Ingo greeted them all with an indulgent schnauzer sigh.

Looking back, I can see that his attitude was based on a terrible misconception. Ingo took consolation in the erroneous view that her stay would be a brief one. After eight weeks a couple of strangers would arrive, hand over a cheque and take her away in a cardboard box, never to be seen again. After all, that's what had happened to him.

When it became clear that this practice wasn't to be followed, Ingo's behaviour changed. When the baby cried, he emitted a mournful yowl. When commanded to be quiet, he would stop and look up at us with sad, brown eyes, a victim of gross injustice: 'You don't tell her to shut up.'

When visitors arrived he no longer waited to be sought out but hurled himself at them with attention-seeking vigour. Male friends started to approach our house sideways, hands cupped in front of their genitals like footballers in a defensive wall, in an attempt to ward off the impact of a high velocity canine skull.

Dogs seek a quiet life. When not in action they want peace and tranquillity. A secure dog lies down and sleeps, conserving its energy for hunting. When well-fed and safe a wolf will sleep for three days at a stretch. What would be the sign of depression in a human is a sign of contentment in a canine.

A house with a baby in it is not a reassuring place for a dog. A baby creates noise and commotion. The parents are always rushing about. There is juice and food to be fetched, and then a cloth to mop up the juice and food. The baby yells and cries and tries to kill itself by all means possible. It wakes up at all hours. The TV is on at 4 a.m. with all the family sitting on the carpet singing the theme from *Pingu*. The dog is sent into a state of almost nervous collapse by all the activity. When Mum or Dad jump up, he feels compelled to jump up too. He follows them about. Every time they turn round they trip over him and shout in irritation. Poor Ingemar got yelled at an awful lot. In fact, the first complete sentence our daughter uttered was, 'For Heaven's sake, get out of the way, you stupid animal!'

Dogs are snobs by nature, adoring those who are above them in the hierarchy. Once Maisie started to issue commands, I imagined Ingo's attitude to her would begin to soften. Just after lunch, when she was two, he actually licked her face. This was surely a sign of affection, I thought. But then I realised it was nothing of the sort. It was just that she had been eating spaghetti bolognese and there was mince stuck to her chin.

Ingemar, in fact, was stoic. Faced with changes he did not like, but could do nothing about, he simply ignored the cause of them. That which cannot be altered must be endured. Maisie and Ingo lived in the same house for eight years but he never once acknowledged her existence. We got her to give him biscuits and put down his food bowl. It made no difference to his attitude. 'Where's Maisie?' we would say to him when we were in the sitting room and she was elsewhere in the house, 'Where's Maisie? Go and find Maisie.' We'd use our best breathy, excited, this-is-a-game voices, but it had no effect. Ingo simply sat staring at us blankly: 'Maisie? Nooooo, I don't think I recognise that word.'

A cormorant sat on a rock over by the far bank. It was holding its wings out to dry giving it the impression of a miniature mutoid version of the *Angel of the North*. The cormorant is not pleasant to look at. There is something disturbingly pre-historic and reptilian about it. Perhaps that's why it is arguably the most derided bird in the world. It is the only fowl named in the Old Testament as unclean and there are dozens of websites run by fanatical anti-cormorantists, whose ravings at times sound like the deranged outpourings of some Nazi sect. Just about the only people who seem to like cormorants are the Japanese. They use the bird to catch pipefish. The cormorants catch the fish in their beaks, but are yanked back to the surface and forced to cough them up before they can swallow. The regurgitated fish are then served to the Japanese imperial family as a gastronomic delicacy. No wonder Emperor Hirohito always looked so grumpy.

We met Mr Fudgie on the shore of the river, throwing sticks into the water for Fudge to swim for. He looked a bit glum. He said he'd had a call the week before from his mother-in-law. Mr Fudgie's mother-in-law lived in wild west Durham, in a former pit village that had the look of somewhere tumbleweeds might blow through. 'They say it was a one-horse town,' Mr Fudgie said with a grimace, 'until the locals ate it.'

'I answered the phone, right?' Mr Fudgie said. 'And this voice said, "The dog has died. You'll have to do something with it," and – click – put it down again. She's a rare one that woman, I can tell you. So I went over, I said, "So where's this dog?" and she handed me a potato sack with a lump in the bottom of it. She said, "There's a pet crematorium next village over," and – bang – the door shuts in my face. Communication's not her strong suit.'

So Mr Fudgie went to the pet crematorium, which was located on the outskirts of another former pit village. 'Even rougher than the one the mother-in-law's in,' Mr Fudgie said. I knew the village he meant. And I knew it was rugged. When my dad retired he decided to take up fishing again. He wanted to fish on the Tees, but all but one of the angling clubs was full. The one that had vacancies was in the village Mr Fudgie was talking about. When my dad asked one of the blokes from his work what you needed to become a member of the angling club there, the bloke replied, 'A police record and a bull terrier ought to do it.' My dad decided not to bother.

'There were all these characters lurking about by the betting shop, tattooed from head to toe and pumped up on steroids. And that was just the women,' Mr Fudgie said. 'Still, I don't suppose you're going to find a pet crematorium in Knightsbridge, are you?'

The man who came out to greet him when he walked through the doors was like a real undertaker, Mr Fudgie said: dark suit, all soft-voiced and pale and oleaginous. 'And is this . . . the loved one?' the man had asked Mr Fudgie, indicating the potato sack. And Mr Fudgie had said it was.

'Would you like a little time alone with your departed friend in the chapel?' the man had asked. Mr Fudgie had said that on balance he'd probably just prefer to get on with it ('Because, to be honest, there was a bit of a niff'). The crematorium man had patted him on the arm gently, certain that his haste was the sign of genuine welling emotion.

'I wouldn't care,' Mr Fudgie said, 'but, after all that concern and sort of, well, Godliness, when I came out and got back into the car I noticed smoke puffing out of the crematorium chimney and a few seconds after, flakes started floating down out of the sky. It was bloomin' fur,' he said, 'though there was some sack in it too, I should imagine.'

We were staying in a cottage in the Vale of York. It was mid afternoon and I was trying to read the newspaper, but Manny had other ideas. Even though he'd already been out twice, he kept coming and bothering me. He'd wander into the sitting room, put his paws up on my thigh and squeak, then when I made him get down he'd sit and stare at me and if I stared back he'd let out his call: 'Arrrrroooo!'

Manny usually had two walks a day but, the day before, a friend had called round to see Catherine at about 3 p.m. and suggested a walk. So Manny got three walks that day and now he was eager to convince me that this should become a routine. It didn't surprise me, really, because over years of living with dogs I have come to the conclusion that while it takes months and months to teach them a good habit, they can pick up an irritating one in a single go. In fact, I was thinking of declaring this phenomenom Pearson's Second Law of Canines. My father had devised Pearson's First Law of Canines back in the 1970s. It stated that: 'Whenever a door is shut a dog will always be on the wrong side of it.' This was a damn fine law.

'Today only,' I said eventually. 'Then it's back to normal.' Manny faked to run off in the direction of the door, then checked back just to make sure I wasn't fooling with him.

We walked along an old railway line, passed a beech wood and a sign that warned 'Don't be fooled: these animals bite!!!' There were corrugated sheds in the wood but the pigs that had once lived in them had evidently moved on. After half a mile, we cut down an old siding and into an open field. Near a large sycamore tree, Manny stopped suddenly and sniffed at the air. I had seen him do this many times and then been amazed when I followed the direction in which his nose was pointing to catch sight, two hundred yards away, beyond the hedge through which Manny could not see, a fox skulking along, its paws high-stepping daintily, its head hanging low, half dandy and half vagabond. This time, though, when I looked I saw something entirely unexpected – ostriches.

Whatever the ancestry of the big cats which reportedly prowl the north Pennines, they must nowadays feel quite at home. The move toward greater diversification in British farming over the past few decades has left a number of peculiar legacies, including a greater density of holiday cottages than any other nation in northern

Europe and some rather tenuous theme parks in which, among other things, the milking of cows is presented as entertainment.

It has also brought an exotic tinge to the landscape. In the north of England it's not uncommon to turn the corner in a country lane and find yourself confronted by a llama; there are water buffalo in Deepdale and alpacas near Penrith.

The sudden appearance of an ostrich should no longer draw cries of amazement from passers-by, either. The eight-foot-tall, 300-pound ratite from the African veldt is now almost as much a part of the rural scene as those other feathered imports, the pheasant and the pea-cock. You see their bald heads turning inquisitively from left to right, like an elderly housemaster picking up the scent of cigarettes, everywhere from the Eden Valley to Pickering.

Though the ostrich has many things to recommend it from a farming point of view (it matures quickly, offers income not only from meat but also from leather, feathers and eggs, and breeding females remain productive for more than forty years), many members of the public find the birds gross and unappealing.

There is something about all that bare, pale, pimply flesh that conjures up unpleasant memories of a chilly August bank holiday on Redcar Sands (but the discovery that ostriches are dull-witted, easily stressed and have poorly developed pectoral muscles has left others feeling an odd empathy for them). Perhaps this is why organisations such as the British Domestic Ostrich Association have had a bit of a problem persuading British people to buy its low-cholesterol meat, even during the height of the BSE scare. Recently there have been reports of a financial crisis among British ostrich farmers. It wouldn't be the first one.

Ostrich farming began in Ancient Egypt where they were raised not just for food but because the fashionable ladies of the time liked to ride around on them. The Greeks and Romans carried on the tradition. The idea of farming the great bird in Britain is not as newfangled as it might seem. The first ostrich farm was set up here in the 1680s. It didn't last long. In Victorian times, several attempts were made to establish ostriches in the UK. Despite the demand for plumes from the hat trade, all failed.

The weather was usually held responsible. But that seems to have been an easy excuse. Ostriches have been commonplace on the Continent for some while, particularly in Belgium where the passion for covering even the smallest patch of land with grazing livestock sees them turn up in the unlikeliest places. I once saw half a dozen strutting myopically about around the circular pools in the centre of a sewage farm. It was just outside Lessines, birthplace of René Magritte. The great surrealist would surely have appreciated this bizarre juxtaposition.

Whatever your opinion about the ostrich, there are several things everyone knows about them: they can run very fast, they can disembowel a man with a single kick and when frightened they stick their head in the sand. The latter is one of those strange quirks of animal psychology that will perhaps never be explained. After all, if you are well over two metres tall, weigh twenty stone and can rip an assailant's intestines out with one blow, what have you got to be afraid of?

The fourth thing everyone knows about ostriches is that whenever they appear in a cartoon or comic they, at some point, always swallow an alarm clock. This is not as fanciful as it might appear. Ostriches are attracted by shiny objects. According to experts they can pick a pair of glasses off your nose and gulp them down long before you have time to react. So, when you come across an ostrich remember to remove your spectacles (and any timepieces you happen to have about your person) before you say hello.

August

We had rented a cottage for a week up on the Northumberland coast. The garden gate opened right on to the beach. On the first morning there were seals splashing in the water, their sleek heads turning quizzically towards us when we went out to take their photos.

I'd thought the beach would be a good place for Manny. I imagined I'd be able to let him off his lead and he'd have a good run about, following the trails left by gulls and sandpipers. But on that first morning I released him and he simply ran in one big circle, lifted his nose in the air and then disappeared over the dunes. I ran after him, yelling frantically, and eventually caught up with him just as he was forcing his body under a mesh fence in an attempt to get into a field filled with sheep. So that was the end of that idea.

Instead we walked along the water's edge, watching families making sandcastles. The families came every day and busied themselves with spades and buckets for hour upon hour. If they'd set their mind to something more permanent, by the end of the week they'd have had a three-bedroom bungalow.

It was clear from my observations that there are three

things that are indispensable when building a sandcastle: sand (obviously), the sea and children. A dog could also be added though, in my experience, while generally useful for excavation work, limited building skills coupled with a tendency to keep running off with the buckets make them a liability.

There are many types of sand, but – at the risk of getting over-technical – the best type for making sandcastles is what experts term 'damp'. This is easy to recognise because it is a darker colour than the dry sort and far less likely to have girls in bikinis lying on it.

While important, the children's function should not be overestimated. They are there for three reasons only:

a) to provide the excuse to build the sandcastle in the first place (because, let's face it, a grown man building a sandcastle on his own is likely to attract some strange looks),
b) cheap labour,
c) to offer the opportunity for frequent fatherly outbursts along the lines of 'Honestly, Noah, don't they teach you anything about the military engineering of Marshal Vauban at school?', 'When I was in year six, I had committed the entire British trench line at Ypres to memory', or 'For Heaven's sake, is that what passes for a ravelin these days? Look at your counterscarp; it's all over the place', and so on and so forth.

The castle must be built to some scheme held only in the father's head (because, like coal-mining, the priesthood and burning sausages on a barbecue, this is man's work) and should be explained strictly on a need-to-know basis to the children as fast as he can make it up. A sandcastle can never be too big or too elaborate. In fact, it must continually be a work in progress, expanding to encompass a large patch of beach and an entire morning and afternoon.

It is at this point that the sea comes in. The sandcastle must always be situated so that just as it looks like it is finally about to be finished it will be washed away by the tide. This event will generally incense the children, who will point out that if Father had followed their advice and built it higher up the beach it would still be standing as a testament to their ingenuity and hard work.

This should not put Father off, however. In fact, he should relish the moment, saying, 'Yes, well, I think you'll find that was actually part of my plan. You see, we have all learned an important lesson today about the transience of human achievement. *Sic transit gloria mundi*. Or as the immortal Percy Shelley so memorably wrote: "My name is Ozymandias, king of kings: Look on my works, ye Mighty, and despair! Nothing beside remains . . . Er, uhm, de-dum-de-dum, colossal wreck, er, boundless and bare the sands stretch far away etc., etc." Well, to your way of thinking that may sound totally random, Oliver, but I can assure you that it is not.'

Father will then reinforce his message about hubris and futility by buying everybody enormous ice creams just so long as they stop being in a mood and cheer up a bit, for goodness' sake. We're supposed to be on holiday, after all.

As Manny and I strolled along listening to all this chatter a Weimeraner suddenly came rushing through a gap in the dunes, saw Manny and immediately began to trot towards us, hackles raised, head held low. The Weimeraner had grey fur so pallid and shiny there was an almost spectral glow to it. Its eyes were pale too. If a cowboy in a spaghetti Western had those eyes you'd know instantly he was psychotic. I had an uneasy feeling the same might apply here, and so it proved.

When it was five yards away the dog suddenly picked up speed and came towards us, teeth bared. Manny tried to run but the lead pulled him up short. I tried to put myself between him and the Weimeraner, but got there too late. A split second later and Manny was on his back with the Weimeraner snapping at his throat. The Weimeraner had no collar, so I grabbed it by the scruff of the neck pulled it upright, dragged it a couple of yards and then and flung it as far as I could, aiming a kick at it for good measure. 'Go on, piss off,' I said.

Undeterred, the Weimeraner circled round to the left. Worried that Manny would slip his leash and disappear with the dog chasing after him, I picked him up, holding him high in front of my face. The Weimeraner charged in again. Leaping up, its teeth clacked just below Manny's belly. The Weimeraner is a gun dog and, like all gun dogs, it is supposed to have a soft mouth. This, though, didn't seem to be the best way to put that to the test. I swung round to the left and right to keep myself between Manny and the increasingly frantic attacks of the grey dog.

A cry came from behind me. 'Frederick! Frederick, you bastard!' A woman came running through the same gap in the dunes the Weimeraner had emerged from. She was red in the face, out of breath and her blue raincoat was flapping around her like the wings of a giant bat. 'You bloody, bloody bastard, Frederick!' she screamed as she jogged over to us, looped a choke chain over the dog's neck and tugged it away with a slap round the head.

'I'm terribly sorry. Is your dog unhurt?' the woman said gasping for air. 'I really am terribly sorry. Frederick's not his normal self. We're up here on holiday and he's obviously disorientated.'

Nobody ever loses at cards. If you talk to five men who spent the night playing poker the first will say, 'I did all right; won about twenty quid,' another will say he went away 'about a tenner up', a third will say he got a few bad hands but came out seven quid ahead and the other two will shrug and say 'I broke even'. Just as nobody loses at cards, so you never meet anyone with an aggressive dog. You meet people with dogs that are nervous, skittish, or 'had a bad experience once with something that looked a bit like your one', but you never encounter anyone who says, 'Watch out! He's a testosterone-charged hoodlum who'll take any other mutt by the throat at the first whiff of fear.'

'He won't start a fight, but if another dog starts on him then he'll knack them,' men said, restraining red-fanged Alsatians, wild-eyed collies or butch black Labradors. I wasn't altogether sure they weren't projecting a bit here. They were saying things about their dog they'd have liked to have had said about themselves. 'He's a gentle giant,' they'd say, 'very laid back. But if some dog gets him riled, then by golly, you wouldn't want to be in that dog's shoes.'

In my experience dogs don't make those sorts of judgements. Generally speaking they fight when they feel threatened. Small dogs fight more than big ones because they have more to fear. Ingo fought with any dog he met who was the same size as him or larger. He wasn't aggressive, though. He just had poor eyesight and it made him edgy.

Ingo's method of fighting was, I should add, hugely ineffectual, consisting as it did of him launching himself head on at his adversary and then turning away at the last minute so that he slammed into them sideways. Few dogs seemed impressed by this and he usually came off worst in any encounter.

Like Ingo, most dogs' aggressive intent is all posturing, designed to win a psychological ascendancy without the need to actually hurt or be hurt. There is a lot of snarling and strutting and scuffing and the occasional bit of buffeting and then it's all over. Dogs that are seriously menacing don't generally make any sound. They're quiet, they drop their heads down to below their shoulder blades and they come forward at an easy loping pace, veering away in a slow curve in an attempt to get behind their target. That's why no dog likes having another dog to its rear, even if it's fifty yards away. They don't want to be attacked from behind.

When the Weimeraner disappeared back where it had come from I gave Manny a consoling pat. 'Now, you mustn't hold what happened against him,' I said. 'Remember: it wasn't his fault. Society's to blame.'

When Manny and I came out into the field by the railway track the day after we got back from our holiday, we saw Fudgie up ahead chasing round in circles. The person who was with him was not Mr Fudgie but a woman who, with lightning acuity, I judged must be Mrs Fudgie. Mr Fudgie had mentioned his wife many times in conversation but I had never actually seen her before. In fact I had come to believe that I never would, and that she would be much spoken of but never encountered – like Godot.

Mrs Fudgie was a round lady with big glasses, frizzy henna-ed hair and slightly alarming batik trousers. 'So, you're Harry,' she said when I introduced myself to her.

'Well, Harry, I'll have to tell you something, Harry. I think this will make you laugh, Harry. Although to be honest, Harry it's not really funny, Harry, when you think about it Harry.'

Mrs Fudgie really kept saying my name like that, and whenever she said it she flashed a quick grin at me and nodded her head slightly. I knew Mrs Fudgie had a sales job and I wondered if she had been on some sort of training course where they told you that the best way to win client trust was to call people by their names as often as possible. It was either that or she had a very short memory and had to keep reminding herself who she was talking to. 'The thing that happened, Harry, was that he was stood in our garden calling for the dog, Harry. And you'll never believe it, Harry, but the dog came belting round the corner of the house and right into him, Harry.'

Mrs Fudgie said that the collision had caused severe ligament damage to Mr Fudgie's right calf and he was at home now with it heavily strapped, watching *Food Poker* on the telly. 'Harry, you wouldn't believe it possible, would you, Harry?'

In fact I believed it very possible because something similar had happened to my grandfather. My grandfather loved dogs. He took them for long walks and fed them ice cream cornets. He had always had dogs. As a boy, growing up in the mean streets of Middlesbrough, he and his brothers had had a Staffordshire bull terrier named Turpin that had been the terror of the neighbourhood (though only when sorely provoked, clearly). Later, when my grandfather had inherited Turpin's fearsome mantle, there were mutts and mongrels of every description. In photos of my mother and the family when she was a child there are always dogs milling around. 'That's Gyp, and that's Micky,' my mother said one day when we got the photograph albums out to show Maisie, 'that's Reb and that's, that's . . . Well, I won't say what he was called. He was a big black dog and it was a name people gave to black dogs in those days. You wouldn't call a dog it now. You'd get arrested.'

'Wing Commander Guy Gibson VC had a dog with the same name,' my father said from behind the cricket pages, 'though of course when they show *The Dambusters* on television these days they block it out whenever he shouts for it. There's a gravestone at one of the aerodromes.'

'What was the dog called?' Maisie asked.

'It wasn't a very nice name. I think we'll leave it at that,' my mother said. But Maisie was not so easily deterred.

'Was it a rude name?' she said.

'No,' I said. 'It was a nasty word. It's not a word we say. It's the sort of word you might sometimes have heard on hip hop songs.'

'What,' Maisie said, her eyes wide with a mix of horror and delight, 'motherf—'

'No, not that,' I said quickly. 'The N-word.'

Maisie raised her eyebrows. 'Weird,' she said.

'Yes, well, anyway,' my mother said. 'He was a lovely dog and we were all terribly fond of him. Especially my father. Even after the dog broke his leg.'

What had happened was that one day my grandfather had been out walking Micky and the big black dog on the headlands above the sea. The pair had disappeared and granddad had called for them. The two had sprinted back, racing to be first to return to their master, rounded a corner with the big black dog in the lead, and had run straight into him. My grandfather had been walking towards them and had all his weight on his front foot when the collision occurred. The impact must have been pretty dramatic because part of the fractured bone shot out through my grandfather's trouser leg.

'Bust my leg and ruined a new pair of pants an' all, the little bugger,' my granddad would recall happily in later years.

In light of my grandfather's experience I was always wary around running or playing dogs, especially when they were big. Mr Fudgie had not been so circumspect.

'Eee, Harry, I didn't realise what had happened at first, Harry,' Mrs Fudgie said. When Mr Fudgie had finally managed to haul himself back to his feet and limp into the house he had been a bit vexed with her. He'd asked why she hadn't come out and helped him. She'd said she didn't realise he was so badly hurt.

'Didn't realise I was badly hurt?' Mr Fudgie had screeched. 'What did you think I was doing writhing about on the patio? Practising my bloody break dancing?'

'It was the pain talking, Harry,' Mrs Fudgie said.

Walking along the riverbank, Manny and I met two people coming the other way who looked like cross-country skiers who had forgotten to put on their skis, possibly because it was eighteen degrees and the nearest thing to snow anywhere to be seen was the icing from some carrot cake that I'd neglected to brush off my sweater before we'd set off. They both had a pair of long sticks made from some sort of carbon-fibre fastened to their wrists by loops and they were striding rhythmically forward, fists pumping the air like pistons. Waving a stick around in front of any dog is never a good idea. They either cower in terror making the stick-waver feel like a brute and a blackguard, or bound joyfully forward, grab the stick and attempt to wrestle it from the waver's grasp. Manny took the joyful bounding approach.

'I'm terribly sorry,' I said, after I had managed to drag him away from one of the men, who was wearing those khaki trousers with the zips round the legs so you can convert them to shorts without fuss or scissors. 'It's your walking stick he's after.'

'It's not a walking *stick*,' the man with the zip-off trouser legs said in the smug tone of an Oxford graduate correcting somebody on the pronunciation of Magdalene College, 'it is a walking *pole*. A Nordic walking *pole*,' he added, with a little nod for emphasis. And he and his friend strode off again down the path.

'Not a *stick*,' I said to Manny, 'a *pole*. Note the distinction young fellow and don't make the same mistake again.'

Over the next little while I saw more and more people with Nordic walking *poles*. They were different from the other walkers I met: more earnest, more focused and their gear was shiny and new and had the look of something that was destined to end up as one of those items at a car boot sale that passers-by look at and say 'Eee God, remember when everyone had them?'

That would be a while, though. Because currently Nordic walking is Britain's fastest-growing sport. There are now hundreds of walking instructors employed across the country. I am no little Englander – I'm six foot five for a start – but I can't help thinking that things have gone sadly wrong if the citizens of our once proud nation have to pay Scandinavians to teach them how to put one foot in front of the other.

Nordic walking was invented in Finland to overcome health problems arising from the traditional north European diet of lard and alcohol. It could have been called Lapp jogging, but for some reason this option was passed over.

The key to the sport's success in this country is undoubtedly the fact that it is done using poles. These are guaranteed to appeal to British men on a number of levels. (British women have taken up Nordic walking too, I should add, but for all the right reasons.)

Firstly, they add much-needed equipment. If a sport is to be taken seriously this is vital because without equipment there is no advertising and without advertising there are no magazines and without magazines how are you going to know what equipment to buy?

Secondly, poles have always fascinated the British male. This is clear from other areas of life. For example, women had danced naked on bar tops across Blighty for generations without attracting more than passing interest, but the minute they started doing the same thing with a pole it became a nationwide sensation and clubs sprang up all over the land.

A mistaken belief is that men go to these clubs to watch the women. In fact the women are only there to draw attention to the pole. The men gaze spellbound upon this shining object, muttering: 'That's a hell of a thing. It must be, what, fifteen feet long? It looks like stainless steel and I think it's one piece because I can't see a weld anywhere. I wonder if it's solid or hollow.'

It is said that Nordic walking exercises 20 per cent more muscles than jogging. This is because the poles provide a workout for the arms and upper body. They also provide a workout for the jaw as you tell other Nordic walkers about the new carbon-fibre poles – 25 per cent more strength and spring than conventional materials while still maintaining the lightness of cane – which you bought after reading an article in *Practical Nordic Walking Monthly*.

This may well all be true (or indeed not) but, older readers may recall, the sport of Anglo walking, which was hugely popular in this country during the last century, also involved a pole in the form of a stout walking stick. This also gave the arms and upper body exercise as it was put to its traditional uses: pointing at and wrongly identifying birds, knocking the heads off thistles, rapping the noses of over-inquisitive bullocks, being used as a machine-gun to demonstrate how the walker took out a platoon of Nazi storm troopers single-handedly in Normandy, sword-fighting with small children, poking truculent labourers in the chest before addressing them as 'my man', and rescuing a pair of broken spectacles from a particularly messy cowpat.

It is sad that Anglo walking has been forgotten but not at all surprising because, when it comes to health and fitness, the British are in thrall to anything foreign.

Judo, the sporting equivalent of the grey squirrel, was introduced to these shores as an interesting exotic by post-war PE teachers and has since spread like Himalayan balsam, leaving the shy indigenous species of inappropriately clad wrestlers clinging on only in isolated areas such as Cumbria.

In our leisure centres these days you can take lessons in karate, kung fu and tae kwando, but ask at reception for a session of Cornish cross-buttock and they will show you the door, believe me.

'Nordic walking, indeed,' I said to Manny one day as another group strode past us, sticks flailing, on the track up to the fell. 'People forget that this country once led the world in pedestrianism. The greatest walker of all time was that redoubtable hero of the Georgian age, Captain Robert Barclay. Captain Barclay once walked 1000 miles in 1000 hours on Newmarket Heath. To what end he performed this remarkable feat I am not certain, though I suspect he had probably dropped his house keys.

'Barclay, Manny, as you may know, came from a long line of illustrious walkers. His grandfather was MP for Kincardine and made a habit of hiking to Westminster from his home in Fife for the start of each parliamentary session enriching himself along the way – so the historians assure us – with 'many a prize hat for cudgel play or wrestling'. One is reluctant to sound the well-polished bugle of nostalgia, but frankly it is hard to imagine Gordon Brown behaving in so splendid a manner.

'Captain Barclay's father, it should be remarked, walked less but demonstrated a certain aptitude for feats of strength. Once, when this old gentleman found a stray horse grazing on his land, he expelled the trespasser by the simple method of picking it up and hurling it over a hedge.

'Asked to account for his success as a walker Captain Barclay pointed to a diet of Glauber's cathartic salts, underdone mutton, stale bread and flat ale. No mention of poles of any description, you see?'

But Manny had his nose stuck too deep down a rabbit hole to respond.

I met Mr Dodds on the footpath near the level crossing. He was in the company of a very old and tiny lady who put me in mind of the illustrations in Maisie's copy of the Mrs Pepperpot stories. It turned out that the old and tiny lady was his mother, who was up staying for the week. Old Mrs Dodds was ninety-seven years old. 'And you know something, young man?' she said to me. 'I can still touch my toes.' And she demonstrated, in case I didn't believe her. Old Mrs Dodds wore a rather Edwardian hairpiece that was shaped into a bun and apparently made of horsehair. It sat on her head in the manner of a hat. In the act of touching her toes the toupee slid forwards and to the left. When she was upright again it was covering one eye, giving her a piratical appearance.

Mr Dodds asked what I had been up to and I said that the previous day I had gone to Tow Law to watch a football match. 'Ooh-hoo, Tow Law,' Old Mrs Dodds said with enthusiasm. 'Peacock, you'll have to tell him about the haberdashers,' she said to her son.

This was the first time I had ever heard Mr Dodds' Christian name. Even Tommy, who knew him better than most, popping in at his house for cups of tea and to exchange bedding plants, called him Mr Dodds. I had taken this as a mark of respect. Mr Dodds was a very upright character and a man of no little dignity. Now, however, I wondered if it wasn't just that his given name – Peacock – was a bit, well, odd. I could guess how he'd come by it, however. It had once been a habit amongst Northumbrian couples to give their first son his mother's maiden name. Some friends of ours lived next door to an old chap called Worthington Pringle. For years they'd laboured under the impression that it was a double-barrelled surname until one day when they'd called him Mr Worthington-Pringle for the umpteenth time and he'd gently corrected them, waving away their apologies. 'You can call me Worthington, or you can call me Pringle,' he said, 'but the two together are a bit longwinded, and at eighty-two I haven't got time to waste.'

'Tell him about that haberdashers, Peacock,' Mrs Dodds said. Mr Dodds cleared his throat. He said that he

always thought of two things when anyone mentioned
Tow Law. The first was that when he was a lad there were
some traffic lights there, and they were always on red
when he and his father went through in the farm wagon
on the way to Gateshead mart. He said there was a haberdashers shop next to the traffic lights and that
throughout his childhood and adolescence the window
display had always included an enormous pair of pink
bloomers. When Mr Dodds said the last word he exag-
gerated the first syllable, 'blooooooomers'. 'Every time
we stopped there, week after week, month after month,
year after year, winter, spring, summer and autumn,
there they were in pride of place, these enormous pink
blooooooomers,' he said. Mrs Dodds chuckled. Then he
went away and did his National Service in Aden and
when he came back the haberdashers had closed down
and the bloomers had gone. 'I can't say I was that enam-
oured of them,' Mr Dodds said, 'but I wouldn't have
minded one last glimpse for old time's sake.'

The other thing Mr Dodds recalled about Tow Law
concerned his son. A few years back, when Mr Dodds
was having trouble with his car, his son, who was an
engineer down south, had been up visiting. His son said
that he had heard there was a good mechanic in Tow
Law and that he would take the car over there and get
it seen to. Mr Dodds' son, who was then in his late thirties,
took the car up to Tow Law one Wednesday morning.

The mechanic had a look at it and said that he could
see straight away what the trouble was and that it would
take about an hour to put it right. Mr Dodds' son said that
was great. He said he had noticed there was a pub across
the road and he would pop across and have a pint and
come back and collect the car. When he mentioned the

pub the mechanic frowned. 'Well,' he said, 'you can go in there if you like, but I should warn you it has a reputation as a fighting pub.'

Mr Dodds' son thanked him for the heads-up and walked over to the pub. He reckoned it was Wednesday lunchtime, what trouble could he possibly encounter? Mr Dodds' son opened the door of the pub tentatively and peeped in. It was entirely deserted save for three old-age pensioners who were sitting in a corner playing dominoes. 'Looks safe enough,' Mr Dodds' son thought and he walked in and stood beside the bar. The landlord was nowhere to be seen and so Mr Dodds' son stood waiting to get served. After a few minutes one of the old codgers came and stood next to him, three pint glasses held between his hands.

Eventually the landlord appeared behind the bar. 'Sorry to keep you, gents,' he said. 'What can I get you?' And the old codger shoved the glasses at him and said, 'Three pints.' After the landlord had gone off to fill them, Mr Dodds' son turned to the old codger and said, 'I think I was first,' and the old codger stared him straight in the eye and snarled, 'Oh, aye, and d'you want to make something of it?'

Old Mrs Dodds guffawed loudly at this tale. She said that when she was younger she had been a schoolteacher. Her first job had been taking charge of a class of forty infants in the Cannon Street area of Middlesbrough. That was in 1913. Cannon Street was one of the roughest areas in the town and, to be frank, nobody was ever going to mistake Middlesbrough for Cheltenham to start with.

The winters were very cold with icy winds whipping up the Tees, and the children were so susceptible to chills that in the autumn mothers would rub their children's chests with goose fat and then sew them into their woollen vests. She said the treatment was highly effective, but she was glad she'd never been there in the spring when they unpicked the stitches. 'Imagine what that must have smelled like,' she said with a throaty chuckle.

Old Mrs Dodds' favourite story from her teaching days involved a schools' inspector from London paying a visit to an infant school she was teaching at in Crook, County Durham. The schools' inspector was an unctuous man with a religious bent. At the end of the day he offered a penny to the first child who could answer the question, 'Who threw Daniel into the lions' den?' The class stared at him blankly. 'Come on now,' the schools' inspector chivvied, 'You'll win a penny. Why are you not answering?'

'Nay bugger knars, sir,' a small boy at the front of the class volunteered.

The schools' inspector smiled, patted the lad on the head and handed him the coin. 'Quite right,' he said. 'Though in the south of England we pronounce it "Nebuchanezer".'

September

Mr Dodds said to take care in the church field because there was a big Texel tup in there 'with a murderous look in his eye'. 'They'll be putting him to the ewes in a week or so,' Mr Dodds said, 'but at this precise minute he's a very, very frustrated fella.'

Mr Dodds said that a ram was not to be taken lightly. In his experience rampant male sheep injured more people than bulls did. 'It's a matter of human psychology,' he said. 'Folk will flee from a charging bull. But they are altogether more reluctant to be seen running away from a charging sheep.'

I knew the tup he was talking about. It had once spent a winter quartered in the field at the bottom of our garden. It was built like a front-row forward, with massive shoulder muscles and heavy flanks, and wore a permanent scowl. Its eyes were tiny, dark and filled with unfathomable belligerence. Ingo had been particularly keen to make the tup's acquaintance. One day it was standing right next to the gate when we came past and Ingo strained at his leash to get at it. The tup watched him beadily. When Ingo got to within three feet it took a single step away from him and then launched itself forward, butting the steel gate with such ferocity that when we came back a few minutes later it was still vibrating.

'Like the ram, I retreat only that I may butt harder,' I said to Ingo as we walked away. I was quoting Philip of Macedon, father of Alexander the Great, but Ingo wasn't much interested in the Classics. And after the incident with the gate he showed remarkably little interest in the big Texel tup too.

When he used to farm, Mr Dodds said he had a Suffolk tup named Bramwell. Bramwell was a massive black-faced beast as solid as a dumper truck. Like all Suffolks, Bramwell had no horns, but that didn't matter because his forehead was as hard as granite. Once, when the animal had cornered him in a pen and been advancing menacingly towards him, Mr Dodds – fearing a broken thigh – had seized a heavy yard brush and smashed it on Bramwell's head and Bramwell 'just shook himself as if a midgie had bitten him' and kept on coming.

Mr Dodds said that Bramwell had been getting older and they'd thought that every year would be his last. 'We'd put him to the ewes and think, "There's no way he'll cover them all this season,"' Mr Dodds said. But every year Bramwell had performed his duties thoroughly and manfully. 'Mind, it took more and more out of him,' Mr Dodds said. One year, when the paint marks on their rumps showed that Bramwell had completed his job, Mr Dodds had gone to look for the tup, but couldn't see him anywhere. Fearful that the old boy might finally have collapsed and died from his exertions he called for his two young sons to come and help with the search. They eventually found Bramwell at the bottom of a narrow cut, lying on his back on some damp ground, stiff as a board, with his legs sticking straight up in the air. 'I thought he'd pegged out,' Mr Dodds said, 'but when we got nearer we could hear this funny puttering sound, like somebody running a two-stroke engine.' It was Bramwell snoring. He wasn't dead. He was fast asleep. 'Absolutely ruddy jiggered,' Mr Dodds said with a chuckle.

Little Man was scooting along in the field by the river, in eager pursuit of a couple of big rooks. The rooks had been busy with a rabbit carcass and they were not keen to leave their repast, so every time Manny drove them off they flew low in a long loop, came round behind him and landed on it again.

Further up the road somebody had placed a handwritten sign: 'Please Don't Shoot The Rooks,' it read. 'They are interesting and intelligent birds and provide us with many hours of pleasure.' I didn't think the gamekeeper would take much notice.

When Manny and I came to the brow of the hill we saw a woman on a horse about ten yards down the road from us. The horse, a large bay hunter, was flicking its head up and down. There was foam on its flanks. The rider was trying to encourage it to go forward, but whenever she dug her heels in and chucked the reins it stamped its hooves and slid sideways across the road. I wasn't sure whether to approach the horse or not. I have always maintained that I dislike horses, but the truth is I'm fearful of them. They are altogether too large and powerful. I have never come across a dog I was afraid of, no matter how large or vicious it seemed. I always felt you could reason with a dog. I wasn't so sure about horses. Besides, a dog could only do you serious harm if it really, really wanted to, whereas a horse – or so it seems to me – could quite easily kill you by accident.

Up ahead of me the horse whinnied and snorted and bucked. Its eyes rolled, showing a flash of white. It was plainly petrified of something. 'Can I help?' I shouted. The rider turned in the saddle.

'Well, yes,' she said. 'There's a carrier bag stuck in the hedge down there. It's flapping in the breeze and spooking him. Do you think you could get it down on the way past?'

I said that I could. I picked Manny up. I felt having him skittering around was hardly going to improve the situation and, walking as quickly as I felt I safely could without looking a total poltroon, I edged past the horse and strode off down the road to where the plastic bag was flapping from a hawthorn bush. I pulled it off and stuck it in my pocket. As I walked away I saw the horse was following. By the time we had gone fifty yards it had come abreast of us. 'Thanks,' the rider said. 'He's got a totally irrational terror of bags, the silly old thing.'

Funnily enough Ingo had also had a mortal dread of strange carrier bags. If we came across one stuck to barbed wire his hackles would rise and he'd stand stock still for a moment, before beginning to do that thing dogs do when they're frightened – apparently straining forwards and barking menacingly while simultaneously bouncing backwards. I regard it as the cowardly canine's equivalent of the moonwalk.

This was a bit odd as otherwise Ingo was more or less totally fearless. When he was young he and I had been walking along a path at the bottom of a steeply sloping field. A herd of two dozen black and ginger bullocks appeared at the top and watched us suspiciously. Then one of them jumped in the air and they all came hurtling down the hill towards us. I shouted and waved my arms at the cattle but they had too much momentum to stop, so I decided to clamber over the dry stone wall behind me, just to be on the safe side. Ingo was standing about twenty yards away when the stampede started. I called for him to come but he ignored me, staring intently up the hill at the advancing herd. The cattle continued to thunder down the slope so, abandoning Ingo to his fate I scaled the wall. When I dropped down to the other side I peeped back expecting to see a mangled schnauzer. Instead I saw the bullocks running back up the hill with Ingo in hot pursuit. They'd done three laps of the field before I eventually managed to collar him.

When we were out on our regular morning walk, however, anything we encountered that had not been there the day before – a fallen branch for instance, or a strange car parked in an unusual place – made him jumpy and suspicious. Somewhere I'd read a theory that dogs and other animals had a view of the world that in people would be a sign of asperger's syndrome. Even the slightest alteration to a familiar scene set alarm bells ringing, because any change to the environment might indicate the presence of a predator, or of prey.

Though Little Man held a rigid adherence to his daily routine, refusing to eat his suppertime biscuit until after he'd been out for his last perambulation of the day, he showed no fear of either fertiliser sacks or fallen branches. He paid little attention to visuals. Smell was for him the key to understanding his world. Sometimes he'd stop on a walk and refuse to go any further, stiff-legged, head high, his nose damp and nostrils twitching. What it was that had aroused his sense of self-preservation was fathomless to a human. 'Better turn round then should we?' I'd say on such occasions. And Manny would gratefully follow my lead, walking quickly away, glancing back nervously over his shoulder.

*

I walked Manny along the back lane. I was feeling a bit depressed. In that day's edition of our weekly newspaper alongside the usual headlines ('Sack Fell Off Lorry', 'Local Man Shouted', 'Drunk Held Up Daffodil') was an announcement that the local cinema was going to shut down. The cinema was owned by a gentleman well known in the local community largely because of his eccentric dress sense. He looked like he'd stepped right out of an advert for male grooming products circa 1973. The cinema owner had a pageboy hairdo and a Van Dyke beard. He wore jumbo-collared shirts, suede bomber jackets and Crimplene flares and moved around in a cloud of aftershave. And you didn't need to be Hannibal Lecter to recognise it instantly as 'Denim' – the masculine fragrance for men who don't have to try too hard.

The cinema owner was also the cinema projectionist and the cinema box-office assistant. After he'd taken your money, he punched the tickets out of the machine and then tore them in half because, as well as being the projectionist and box-office assistant, the cinema owner was also the cinema's usher. He then gave you your change, counting it out in that old-fashioned way: 'Two threes are five, one five is fifty and fifty makes four pounds and one make five and five makes ten.' That at least was what it sounded like. If you actually listened it quickly became apparent that while he was giving you the correct change he was more or less calling out the figures at random. 'Four twos are fifteen, one seven is twenty and twenty makes two and four make seven,' he said.

Some believe the individual has made little difference to the sweep of history. That it is broad social and political trends that determine humanity's twisting course rather than the deeds of men such as Napoleon

Bonaparte. I do not know whether this is true, but I doubt anybody who has lived in the English countryside would countenance it.

My parents grew up in a North Yorkshire ironstone mining village, which was small, but sufficiently isolated to support a cinema. The cinema was run by the ferocious Mr Skippon, a man of such propriety that he used to don a top hat and tails for the evening performances. For children's matinees he adopted a slightly less elegant approach. Once the film had begun he locked the exit door and allowed natural selection to take its course. Some of the more sensitive bairns naturally tried to escape from the ensuing melee, but the owner refused exit to any who couldn't furnish a reasonable excuse.

The most notorious delinquent in the village was a stuttering tough-boy named 'Shedder' Harland. I cannot recall exactly how Shedder had come by his nickname, nor, since I have just eaten a hearty lunch, have I tried particularly hard to do so. Shedder came from a notorious local family; he was to my parents' village what the Dowling lad would be to ours. He was tough but simple and had a terrible stammer. Many years later, when prison had tempered his waywardness, he would tell my dad, 'I just want a new lamp for my b-b-b-bike, Tony, then I'm going straight.' One weekend the young Shedder went to the closed door of the cinema during an episode of *Flash Gordon* and demanded to be let out. 'Who is it and what do you want?' the owner barked.

'It's Sh-Sh-Sh-Shedder and I want a sh-sh-sh . . .' the door opened before he could complete his sentence. I too grew up in a North Riding village (not the same one as my parents, I might add). On my first visit to the cinema in the nearby town, a policeman had to be called midway

through *Zulu* to expel some local youths, who had joined
in with the African warriors' chanting-and-stamping routine so enthusiastically that a piece of ornamental cornice
had come loose and brained the woman from the bike
shop. When I moved back to the northern countryside
after a decade in London, one of the first things I did was
visit the local cinema. *Dances With Wolves* was showing.
Everything proceeded normally until the tender moment
when Kevin Costner first kisses Stands-With-Fist, at which
point the seats around erupted in a peal of giggles and
boyish cries of 'Aw, yeeeeeerch!' I was massively cheered.
I had had inner doubts about the wisdom of leaving the
capital, but this, I knew, was home. Monday was half-
price night. Catherine and I went every week. The films
were generally mainstream Hollywood. For seven years I
saw every film Tom Cruise made. I hate Tom Cruise, but
at £1.20 it was cheaper than staying at home with the fire
on. And besides, the main feature was only part of what
merits the term 'total cinematic experience'. There were
the usherettes with their torches and trays of ice creams,
the moment when the film juddered to a halt and caught
fire, the cries of anguish from little kids who had gone to
the toilet and got lost in the darkness and, best of all,
there were the adverts for local pubs ('Convenient for the
A69!') and estate agents ('Buying and selling houses – it's
what we do!'), and one for a carpet shop featuring a young
woman in a white polo neck rubbing her hands across the
rich wool twist of a Wilton with such a look of ecstasy on
her face it suggested she was experiencing the tactile
marvel of high-quality pile under the influence of mind-
expanding drugs.

Best of all was The Plumbing Advert. The Plumbing
Advert featured a grey-haired man in brown overalls

self-consciously flushing toilets, fiddling with faucets and waggling his plunger to the accompaniment of some funky brass-heavy cop-show jazz. At the end he is presented with a mug of tea by a beaming woman in a pinafore dress apparently fashioned from 1970s wallpaper, while a baritone voice oozing the treacly charm of a practised gigolo asking a dowager to foxtrot announces: 'Brian Hood. Whether it's a dripping tap or a complete central heating system, we'll take care of all your plumbing needs.'

When my friend Will wanted a new boiler fitted, he phoned Brian Hood. He left a message on the answering machine. 'I got your number from the cinema ad,' he said. Brian never returned his call. Fame can do funny things to people.

And now the cinema was closing down. It wasn't unpopular; far from it. Turning up twenty minutes before the start of the programme was often not enough to get you into a film. Even one starring Whoopi Goldberg. It's simply that the 1974 man had decided it was time to retire. Now if we want to see a film we have to make a round trip of sixty miles. Just as the Harlands or the Barlows could personally create a village crimewave, so the onset of old age in one man has dented the cultural life of a community. It's hardly Napoleon, admittedly. Though I have come to regard the unprecedented five-week run of Kevin Costner's *The Bodyguard* as my personal retreat from Moscow.

When Little Man and I came back from our afternoon walk there was a large family kicking through the leaves under the big horse chestnut tree on the corner, looking for conkers, or cheggies as we used to call them where I grew up. When she was little Maisie and I used to spend the wait for the school bus doing much the same thing.

'When you get home we can play conkers,' I said the first time we did it.

'What's that?' Maisie asked.

'It's a game,' I explained. 'What you do is punch a hole in the conker with a screwdriver, thread it on a shoelace and then you whack another person's conker with your conker until you've smashed it to smithereens.'

My daughter considered me carefully, like a golfer assessing a particularly treacherous fairway. 'Yes,' she said eventually, 'we could do that. Or we could plant them in the garden and watch them grow.' This highlights the essential difference between men and women.

Looking at the cheggies when I got home, I could see that she might have a point. The chestnuts we'd collected were not the fighting kind. They were bulbous and glossy as bodybuilders and, as the great philosopher Nigel Molesworth once observed, 'Successful conkers are always shrivelled and weedy.' Much like jockeys in fact. Though, of course, nobody soaks jockeys in vinegar, bakes them in the oven overnight or coats them with clear nail-varnish to improve their performance. Well, not since the authorities got wind of it, anyway.

Every year just down the road from us in Bardon Mill some enterprising villagers host a big conkers competition, the Roman Wall Championships. The event draws spectators and competitors from across Europe (in France they play a version of the game using snails. Whether garlic butter is also involved I have been unable to ascertain) but not everyone is in favour of it.

A couple of years ago a holiday auction website carried out a poll which revealed that the majority of people in this country are sick of events that paint a picture of us as a nation of lovable eccentrics. The World Conker Championship in Ashton, along with the Coopers Hill Cheese Rolling and the Egremont Gurning contests, were singled out for particular opprobrium. According to a site spokesman, 'With British culture degenerating to game-show level, it is hardly surprising that Britons feel humiliated.'

While there is a self-conscious wackiness about these events that can be irritating (how many more times do we need to see prop forwards from the local rugby club dressed as Charlie's Angels before we cry 'Enough!') it has to be said that if the British people find that the World Bog Snorkelling Championships makes them cringe, how must they feel when they see a British heavyweight boxer fight?

Everywhere, though, it seems the game of conkers is under threat. In 2002 scout leaders in Windsor and Eton banned cubs from playing without written consent from their parents because the game was considered too dangerous. While in Norwich a row of horse chestnut trees were cut down because the local council judged the falling cheggies to be a hazard to passers-by. Prince Charles spoke out against the action at the time and rightly so. What kind of society is it that values sharp cognitive faculties more highly than interesting head wounds?

Not that I am unqualified in my support of conker championships. At Bardon Mill they play the 'three hits each' rule. Personally I favour the 'hit till you miss' style, which to my mind gives a more subtle game. All aficionados know that, when it comes to conkers, hitting is much the same as being hit, Newton's third law of motion stating that action and reaction are equal. With 'hit till you miss' the owner of a delicate conker, or one that has been reduced to a shard of shell no bigger than a toad's toupee, can preserve it by administering only the softest of taps to his adversary's nut until darkness or boredom intervene to save him.

Nor does the Roman Wall competition include 'stamps'. An exciting variation, which allows the opponent of anyone whose conker hits the ground to chase after it attempting to crush it underfoot, while the owner scrabbles about on the floor trying to retrieve it and avoid getting his fingers broken.

You might think it unlikely that anyone would drop his conker during competition, but a gifted player can use 'strings' (a shot in which the respective conker laces become entwined) to disarm his adversary with a sudden twirl of the wrist in the manner of D'Artagnan. Or, at least, he can unless his opponent has wound the lace round his fist. In this case any attempt to spin or tug the conker from his grasp simply draws the lace around the knuckles until they are as tight as a tourniquet. On a frosty autumn morning this produces the kind of sharp, icy pain traditionally associated with unrequited love. Or supporting Fulham.

The winning conker, of course, inherits all the previous victories of the defeated nut. If a twoer beats a sixer it becomes an eighter and so on. I can't help thinking this scoring system might profitably be adopted by other sports. Imagine the thrills and drama that would be brought to the English Premiership if the winners not only picked up three points for a victory but also all their beaten opponent's points too. Arsenal certainly wouldn't be talking tough if they knew that defeat at the Stadium of

Light in the last game of the season would condemn them to relegation and propel Sunderland to the title.

Seeing the family gathering conkers under the tree reminded me that we had some German friends coming over later with their two children. The son was eight and I was sure he'd enjoy a game of conkers, so I gathered half a dozen that were lying by the side of the road, took them home and strung them.

When the Germans arrived I took the father and son out into the garden and explained that they were about to experience a true British cultural phenomenon. I showed them the conkers and outlined the rules. I got the son to hold his conker and prepared to demonstrate the art of striking. 'Of course,' I said, as I took deliberate aim, my string wound round my knuckles to give me about nine inches of swing, 'the game is banned across the country now because everyone is so worried about Health and Safety. Ridiculous nonsense. I can't for the life of me see how anyone could get injured playing conkers.'

I then swung the cheggy with considerable force at the dangling target. I missed it by a fraction of an inch and my conker swirled round and completed its arc by smacking into the underside of my wrist. It hurt like hell. For a moment I thought a bone was broken. Though I said nothing about it at the time, obviously.

Manny had been vomiting off and on for several days. Catherine phoned the vet. 'They say they can see him on Wednesday and we have to bring a urine sample.'

'A urine sample?' I asked. 'Do we have to get him to pee in a flask? How are we going to do that?'

Catherine said the vet hadn't told her. So we got a jam jar and lid out of the pantry and left it on the windowsill on the porch. And every time either of us took the dog out we forgot to take it with us.

On the morning of Manny's appointment it fell to me to take him out. 'We've got to get that urine sample,' Catherine said, making good use of what I like to think of as the 'collective we'. (This is as opposed to 'collective I' which was used rather frequently by a shopkeeper for whom I once worked. This gentleman's comment to a customer that, 'I'll just run up to the fourth floor and see if we have one,' was invariably accompanied by a swishing gesture in my direction to indicate that I should head for the stairs.)

'I know,' I said. I had woken up earlier than usual think-ing about this very topic and I had had what I considered a brainwave. The night before we had had a takeaway curry and I had been struck by the usefulness of the flat plastic containers the meal came in. They were about six inches long and four inches wide. I thought it would be much easier to get Manny to hit one of those than the mouth of a jam jar and so I had swooshed the one that had had my prawn biryani in it under the tap, dried it with kitchen towel and put it in the pocket of my dog-walking coat.

I set off down the lane with the dog lead in one hand and the container in the other. My plan was to catch Manny early, put a lid on the container and leave it some-where so I could pick it up on the way back. Getting a dog to pee into a container is no easy task, however. Every time Manny looked like he was about to cock his leg I shoved the container under him and stood back. But seeing me make such an odd action put him off. We walked down the lane, Manny stopping every ten yards to sniff a likely tussock of grass, me placing the curry container under him and Manny looking at me suspiciously and then moving off again. By the time we had gone four hundred yards it had become obvious to me that this was not going to work. I decided to wait until Little Man was in mid flow before placing the container. This was much more successful, though by the time I had collected a small pool of urine in the bottom of the container I had got considerably more of the warm liquid on my hands and my sleeves. I put the lid on the container. I wiped my hands and cuffs with my handkerchief, and put my handkerchief in the outside pocket of my coat. By now we had gone well past the point in the walk where it was possible for me to leave the container behind, so instead I was compelled to carry it with me.

Manny and I wandered on through the semi-darkness accompanied by the occasional screech of a barn owl and the far off baying of the hunt foxhounds which were kennelled on a nearby fell. When we walked through the lych gate of the church I noticed a light was on in the vestry. I hustled Manny past. It was coming up to Harvest Festival and the last thing I wanted was the Vicar coming out, seeing the carton in my hand and thinking I'd come to make a contribution.

Just after we'd negotiated that potential hazard I sneezed and instinctively took out my hankie and blew my nose. It was only when I put it back in my pocket I noticed the strong ammonia scent that had now attached itself to my nostrils. 'Great,' I said to Manny. 'I've got dog pee on my hands, dog pee on my sleeves, dog pee in my pockets, dog pee on my face and I'm carrying a plastic box filled with dog pee. Let's just hope we don't meet the Queen, shall we?'

When I got home Catherine was standing by the stove

making tea. 'I have the urine sample,' I called, tri-
umphantly brandishing the curry container. Catherine
eyed it suspiciously.

'Did you wash that out thoroughly?' she asked.

'Of course,' I replied.

'Only,' she said, 'it looks a bit yellow.'

'Well, naturally it looks yellow,' I said. 'It is, after all, dog
piss.'

I decanted Manny's sample into a small jam jar.
Catherine took it with her to the vet. The vet said that
Little Man was fine, though his urine did contain higher
than the usual levels of turmeric.

Catherine and Maisie had gone shopping and they had
dropped me off at the park by the river. The park was normally pretty quiet, but today the fair had arrived and there
was a tumult of clanking steel, roaring generators and
Europop.

As a boy, I approached life as if it were a mountain,
charting my course from one holiday camping ground to
the next, scaling the implacable rock face of the scholastic
year using the well-marked toeholds of weekends, half-
terms and special occasions – my birthday, Bonfire Night,
the annual school trip to Flamingoland. Stokesley Fair in
North Yorkshire was held a couple of weeks into the long
autumn term. Throughout the dog-end days of the school
holiday, I could see Stokesley Fair protruding, a friendly
outcrop on the formidable cliff of algebra, hymn practice
and charred liver that loomed ahead of me.

As fair week approached I would begin to pester my
parents. What night would we go on? My mother
demurred. 'We'll have to see,' she said. She said this every
year. My parents did not share my excitement about

Stokesley Fair. I put this down to their warped sense of financial priorities. Parents were strange creatures when it came to money, ever willing to waste hundreds of pounds on non-essentials such as furniture and carpets, yet reluctant to part with even a couple of quid to secure such life-altering items as a Johnny Seven machine gun with realistic flashing barrel. Later I would come to see that my parents' lack of enthusiasm for the fair stemmed from something else entirely.

When you entered Stokesley's cobbled market square in fair week you were assailed by a smell of diesel oil and frying onions, the noise of pop music, barking PA systems and shrieks from a ride called the 'Dive Bomber'. And beneath it all was a low, percussive thudding that came from the generators, but might just as easily have been the throaty thrum of adolescent hormones.

It was the early seventies and groups of teenage girls in satin hotpants and white eyeshadow, sashayed between the coconut shies and the stalls selling acid-coloured gonks and engraved mirrors, cackling at the cries and wolf whistles of the greasy-denimed gaff lads who manned the rides and the local boys loitering outside the pubs.

There was a mixture here of sex and alcohol and holiday licence which in an ideal world would result in bliss and merriment, but in the real one tended to culminate in someone getting a beer bottle smashed in his face. It was the odour of impending violence that put my parents off Stokesley Fair.

I was a child, however, and all this went over my head. I was dazzled by the fair; by the flashing lights of the waltzers, the fizz of sparks that flew from the ceiling above the bumper cars and the glimmering goldfish in the polythene bags. And I loved the food, which seemed to me the very ambrosia of the Gods, with added ketchup. Admittedly I was ten and my palate was not yet sophisticated. In fact, my ideal meal would have been a quart of American cream soda, a packet of Twiglets and a half-pound box of Milk Tray with all the toffees removed.

Armed with a hot dog, or sugary cloud of candyfloss (called *barbe à papa* in France, incidentally – conjuring an intriguing world of elderly Gallic gentlemen with vivid pink whiskers) we would wander through the Hall of Mirrors, past the fortune tellers' caravans and the House of Wonders. The last was a vestige of the old freak shows that had once dominated English fairgrounds. It boasted Siamese twins, a two-headed calf and a three-legged chicken.

The House of Wonders was misnamed on two counts: first, it was not a house but a tent and second, the only thing of wonder about it was that people would pay money to go in. Not that I ever did go in. My parents refused to countenance it. But schoolmates did and reported disgustedly that the Siamese twins were plasticine, the two-headed calf pickled and the three-legged chicken 'was just a normal chicken with a wooden leg stuffed up its bum'.

After I had finished whatever I was eating it would be time to decide which ride to go on. I was only allowed to go on a certain number. How many I cannot recall, though the figure 'not enough' is the one that sticks in my mind.

Choosing a ride was not as easy as it sounded. This was because my dad worked in the structural steel business and was permanently on the lookout for rides that were built according to sound engineering principles. I don't think he ever found one. Instead he would gingerly seat us on the Octopus of the Moon rocket, muttering the mantra, 'God knows how this got a Health and Safety Certificate,' over and over to himself.

It was on one such ride, the Speedway, that my love affair with fairs came to an end. The Speedway was a kind of macho roundabout featuring fast-moving motor-bikes. I fell off mine, landing on the boarding and staring up at my father, grey-faced and open-mouthed ('Like a baby bird' he would say later). I was physically unhurt but the thrill was knocked out of me. I never went to the fair again.

October

A silver-haired lady with a rather elegant wicker basket was standing by the road picking rosehips. I hadn't seen anyone doing that for a long while. When I was a boy we had been given free rosehip syrup at school during the winter months. That was because rosehips contain twenty times more vitamin C than oranges and, what's more, they cost a lot less. Rosehip syrup, along with that other British childhood vitamin C supply staple, Ribena, had first been developed at the Agricultural and Horticultural Research Station at Long Ashton in Somerset during World War II.

For decades afterwards children could earn a bit of pocket money by collecting rosehips and selling them to the corner shop for tuppence a pound. The shopkeeper then passed them on to the local County Herb Committee who in turn supplied the Vegetable Drug Committee of the Ministry of Supply. (Is it just me or are you suddenly getting visions of elderly men with round, horn-rimmed spectacles and belted gaberdine mackintoshes, sucking on briarwood pipes and saying, 'Take this down to the boffins at HQ, old girl, and see what they make of it'?) At one time 450 tons of rosehips were collected in this way each year.

We used to pick them when I was a child – not for any commercial purpose but because the fibrous 'hairs' that surround the seeds made a fine and particularly unpleasant itching powder that could be dropped down the shirt collar of friends and enemies, causing them to squirm about throughout hymn practice until Mrs Harbottle the music teacher sent them to stand outside the headmaster's office. I didn't suppose this was what the lady with the elegant wicker basket was planning, but Little Man and I gave her a wide berth all the same.

The walk back from the church had taken an extra fifteen minutes because Manny kept bouncing after pheasants. There were dozens of them everywhere. Keith the gamekeeper was out practically every minute of the day, shooing them back to the safety of the woods so they wouldn't get run over before anyone could shoot them.

The pheasants this year were a new lot he'd bought from somewhere in Yorkshire. The previous batch from Cumbria hadn't been popular with the guns. 'Too bloody fast,' Keith said. 'And they took off like a jump jet. Straight up a chimney from a standing start, they'd go.' The guns wanted a challenge but these Lakeland birds made them look stupid. You didn't pay £250 a day to bag a brace of fresh air.

Like many non-indigenous species that thrive in their new environment, the ring-necked pheasant is an adaptable creature. Introduced into the Midwestern states of the USA in the 1880s, it soon became such a feature of the landscape that South Dakota adopted it as the state bird. The South Dakotan burg of Winner styles itself the Pheasant Capital of the World, and such is the prestige of that title that a nearby rival is currently suing the town over its ownership.

I have no idea what the Pheasant Capital of Great
Britain is but, if the award is based solely on the number
of the birds to be seen hopping and flapping about in the
fields or crushed on the roads, then the Northumbrian
village in which I live must be a major contender for the
title. *Phasianus colchicus* is everywhere. 'The sooner they
start shooting these damn things the better,' the locals
mutter each September, swatting brownish mottled clouds
of them away as if they were midgies.

It is hard to disagree with this sentiment, especially
when considering the gaudily coloured and lustfully yodelling cock pheasant. For while the hen is a pleasant creature,
plump, dowdy and gregarious (were she a human she would
be typecast as the heroine's kindly aunt in a Jane Austen
novel) the male of the species is an altogether different
proposition.

Many years ago I visited a smart shoe shop in the
Burlington Arcade to buy a pair of slippers as a gift for my
father. The assistant, a short man with thinning hair, took
one look at me and, breaking off from attending to a
smart middle-aged woman, guided me into what I later
came to realise was the storeroom. 'I'm serving Her
Ladyship,' he hissed reprovingly and then departed, shut-
ting the door and leaving me in semi-darkness among the
spare laces and Scotchguard spray. Only when the aristocrat had been seen safely from the premises did he release
me and enquire what exactly it was I wanted.

I think of this shop assistant whenever I see a male
ring-necked pheasant. It is not so much that they look
alike, though both creatures have mastered the difficult art
of staring down their curved beaks at people considerably taller than themselves, but that their attitudes are so
markedly similar.

The manner of the cock pheasant, as you attempt to shoo him out of your garden where he has been munching your peas, is one of withering disdain. He surveys you with a red-rimmed eye that almost demands a monocle, before strutting imperiously away. He clearly thinks of himself as a nobleman and you as a *dreadful little fellow*. On one count, at least, he is wrong. The pheasant is no toff, though he owes his existence to those who are. His ancestors came here shortly after the Norman Conquest, brought over from the shores of the Caspian Sea as fodder for the gentry. (That other popular game bird, the red-legged partridge, is by contrast a frightful arriviste; his family didn't come here till 1770.) If a guy hangs around with posh people long enough the chances are that pretty soon he will get to thinking that he is posh also.

Nine hundred years is clearly long enough to have convinced cock pheasants that they are lords of all they survey. The only member of my household who could force them to leave the garden was Ingemar the schnauzer. Ingemar was a thoroughbred with an impressive pedigree. I always suspected that it was the fact that one of his Kennel Club names was Charlemagne, rather than his ferocity, that sent the pheasants flapping and squawking over the wall and into the neighbouring woodland. 'Ah yes,' you could practically hear them say as they chucked and cawed among the undergrowth, 'I hear he's one of the Bavarian Charlemagnes. Related to the Habsburgs, by all accounts, on the mother's side.'

Despite my antipathy, I couldn't help feeling a little sorry for the male pheasant when the leaves began to fall. In autumn, his delusions of grandeur are shattered in the most rude and peremptory manner. He regards himself as a member of the nobility. Once the shotguns start blasting, however, he realises pretty fast that he is just another flunky.

The arrival of autumn is a time of mixed emotions, of sadness and consolation. The nights are drawing in, but the lawn no longer needs cutting; the morning air is chill, but it has killed the harvest flies; the swallows have fled, but in the local library the Community Education brochure has appeared in the wire rack, next to the dog-eared copies of *Farming News* and *Horse & Hound*.

I have only ever attended one evening class – in Pitman's shorthand, decades ago when I nursed an ambition to become a journalist (the crazy dreams of youth, eh?) and I have no intention of starting any now. Despite that fact, the programme never passes through my hands unthumbed. It is a document rich in hope, humour and pathos. (Take, for example, a course that promises a practical introduction to finding and buying a home in France – a series of lessons for which those on job seekers allowance or income support are entitled to a discount of £5.50.) More than that, however, the list of classes is a clear indicator of the battle that is currently raging for the hearts and minds of the countryside.

One day I fell into conversation with a man standing next to Manny and me at a barbecue. I had taken Manny with me as an escape clause. When I was a student at a hotel school one of the chef lecturers had begun his demonstration on cooking baked Alaska by asking how many of us smoked. A few hands went up. 'Well, my advice to the rest you is to start immediately,' the lecturer said as he whisked egg whites into stiff peaks, 'because when you are working in a kitchen it is hot and brutal and hard and you will need a break. Now if you say, "Just nipping out for a fag, Chef," nobody will mind. Whereas if you say, "Just nipping out to stand in the fresh air doing sod-all for five minutes, Chef," you will get a size-ten boot up your backside.' Aside from on health grounds, this was very good advice.

In other circumstances, a dog performs a similar function to a cigarette. Whenever I have to go somewhere I don't really want to go I always take a dog. And when things get oppressive or boring it is strange how often I am overwhelmed by the sudden sense that my dog is in desperate need of exercise.

I learned this technique from my grandfather. When my grandmother and her sisters got together and the air in my grandparents' front room filled – as it inevitably did – with the scent of lavender water and talk of surgical procedures, my granddad would suddenly hear, above the noisy recounting of sinus scrapes and gall bladder removals, the sound of his dog, Rebel, scratching at the backdoor to be let out. Often the sound was so faint as to be more or less imperceptible to everyone else, but my granddad's ears were finely attuned to the needs of his dog. So finely attuned, indeed, that often he could hear Rebel scratching even before it happened.

Little Man was standing beside me at the barbecue. I knew he would not put up with inertia for long. Half an hour was his limit. Then I'd have to excuse myself (and nobody would mind, of course, because it was the dog, not me, that wanted to leave) and by the time I got back the whole thing would be more or less over and I could go home.

And so for the time being I was talking to this man. I wouldn't normally have started talking so readily to a total stranger but, frankly, it seemed like the only alternative to eating the food. In accordance with some ancient custom, the cooking was being done by a man with absolutely no culinary skills whatsoever in a comedy apron. I had just cut into one of his sausages. Matt black on the outside, it was still a raw, ruddy pink inside. Every time I looked down at my plate I thought of a frogman after a shark attack.

The man standing next to me had no such problem, having side-stepped botulism by plumping for a vegetable kebab. He and I chatted away amiably until I mentioned something I had seen on TV. 'Oh,' he said, giving me the pained look of someone betrayed. 'You have a television, then?'

I nodded. 'Why?'

'Well,' he said, waving a hand vaguely in the direction of the open fields beyond the fence of the garden, 'people who choose this way of life often make a conscious decision *not* to have one.'

The man had clearly misjudged me. My partner and I moved to the country because we were sick of being woken up at 3 a.m. by our next-door neighbours having sex. We weren't making a statement. Or, at least, if we were it was simply, 'We can't stand the sound of that woman at number forty-six groaning ecstatically for a moment longer.' A declaration that seems unlikely ever to become the rallying cry of a generation. What he said was probably true for many other recent arrivals in the distant Shires, however; people who have come determined to forge an alternative lifestyle in the midst of a very conservative one.

Nowadays, in the streets of any English market town you will find fishing tackle suppliers and gun shops next to stores selling crystal prisms and CDs of Native American chanting. I pointed this out to a friend of ours recently. 'It shows how diverse life is here,' she said. That would be one interpretation. A less optimistic verdict might be that it shows how divided things are.

Nowhere are the battle lines better demarcated than in the range of night classes offered by the Community Education Programme. Here, amid the IT, accountancy and conversational Spanish courses, the forces of tradition butt up against the new and the mystical. Man in the Kitchen stands beside Feng Shui ('When energy can't flow it stagnates. Please bring a packed lunch'), Découpage battles for public attention with T'ai Chi, Marquetry with Reflexology, Stickdressing with Raqs Sharqui – Dance of the East.

Of course, when diametrically opposed cultures live side by side they have the habit of cross fertilising. Just as white hillbilly music merged with black rhythm and blues to form rock 'n' roll in the Deep South, so in the future might flower arranging pollinate aromatherapy. Then perhaps I will open my local Community Education Programme brochure and find somebody teaching Lathe Work – The Yogic Way, Men in Belly-Dancing (Intermediate) or Tantric Sugarcraft. Though clearly I'd settle for Competent Cook behind the Barbecue.

When Manny and I came round the corner by the big sycamore tree we saw Keith the gamekeeper. He was standing bent over the engine compartment of his six-wheeled buggy. Raffie, his springer spaniel, was sitting on the platform at the back. Raffie, like many spaniels, has a distinctly aristocratic air. He holds his nose high and his eyes have a drooping, mournful quality that put me in mind of Van Dyck's portraits of Charles I.

'The bloody fan belt's snapped,' Keith said. 'Could you give us a hand pushing it down the road?'

The gamekeeper said the buggy was a lot heavier than it looked, and he was right. The two of us heaved and shoved the vehicle along the back lane. Rain began to fall. Our feet slipped in the mud. We grunted and strained. The rain got heavier. Sweat ran down my brow. I could feel dampness spreading through the armpits of my shirt.

'Oh, I say, haugh, haugh, haugh!' Mrs Pelham-Beale had come over the stile with Benbow under one arm and had been watching our exertions.

'Well, what a sight,' Mrs Pelham-Beale said, with a nod towards the keeper's dog. 'If little green men are watching from outer space they'll know who's in charge down here, won't they?' I looked up and there was Raffie, still sitting on the platform, eyeing me with kindly condescension.

After we had manoeuvred the buggy to safety I walked down the road with Mrs Pelham-Beale. Mrs Pelham-Beale said that the regal position of the gamekeeper's spaniel had rather reminded her of Benbow in his gilded youth. She said that Benbow was now too old for adventure, but that he had once been quite the young blade. He had got into numerous scrapes, including being carried away in a dustbin wagon, making a guest appearance in the Christmas window-display of Harrods department store and bursting out of a picnic hamper at the Henley Regatta. And then there had been the business with the Wimbledon strawberries and the incident with the former cabinet minister. He had, Mrs Pelham-Beale said, seen the inside of more British police stations than Ronald Biggs.

Despite all this, Benbow rarely got into trouble. He crossed thunderously busy roads, sauntered through some of the country's roughest districts and breached top-level international security measures without ever coming to the slightest harm. Benbow might have been little and wheezy, but he had the overpowering self-confidence of a gentleman. It surrounded him like an impregnable force field. And when apprehended by the authorities he would invariably escape censure by exercising his upper-crust charms. No one, not even the most malign dog-hater, was immune.

Once, Mrs Pelham-Beale said, she had been visiting her sister who – contrary to all advice – had married a man from the south of England, and lived on a country estate next to one of the royal golf courses in Berkshire. Benbow had, as was his wont, disappeared one afternoon. They had searched all over for him, giving particular attention to the larder and the linen baskets, but could find no trace. At 6 p.m. the telephone rang. It was the steward of the golf club. One of the members had found Benbow in a bunker next to the fourteenth green. Mrs Pelham-Beale drove round to the clubhouse to collect him.

The golf club was a strict and starchy place, well known throughout the country for its old-fashioned regulations on membership, dress and etiquette. Mrs Pelham-Beale anticipated a lecture on dog care and responsible owner-ship. Instead, a well-shaved gentleman in a Dunhill blazer, who introduced himself as the secretary of the club, greeted her. 'Benbow is in my office,' he said with a smile, ushering Mrs Pelham-Beale into a clubhouse that women had been forbidden to enter up until five years before and through to a large, oak-panelled room where Benbow was fast asleep, wrapped in a plaid rug on a red leather wing-backed chair. 'I hope you don't mind,' the secretary said, 'but Benbow seemed rather cold and hungry when they brought him in, so I gave him a hot-water bottle, some warm milk and a little plate of smoked salmon.'

'Smoked salmon!' Mrs Pelham-Beale exclaimed in astonishment.

'I know,' the secretary had said. 'But you see, he rather turned his nose up at our ham.'

'Coddled in cashmere and dining on caviar!' Mrs Pelham-Beale said, casting an affectionate beady eye over her pug. 'There's no doubt that this little fellow has a talent for falling on his feet.'

There was a good deal of coming and going up by the cricket field. It was the day of the Vegetable and Produce Show. This was a big day in the village because it was the first show that had been held there for some while. Four years before, the Leek Club in the village had announced that it was closing down due to lack of interest. It was a bitter blow. Every year, from early September to late October, the pages of the local papers in Northumberland and County Durham carry adverts for dozens of leek shows organised by societies based around pubs, allotments or social clubs. From now on, there would be one fewer. The demise of the rural post office, the fox hunting ban and the closure of branch-line stations may draw more publicity but, for many in the region, the cancellation of a leek show was the sign that life in the English countryside had truly reached rock bottom.

You see, while the leek may be the national emblem of Wales, it is in the land between the Tweed and the Tees that growing *Allium porrum* is really taken seriously. The pastime began in the late nineteenth century among coal miners and shipyard workers looking for a cheap hobby and something extra to eat. Over time, as the leeks grew

bigger so did the stakes. Nowadays, obtaining membership of a top leek club was infinitely more difficult than
joining the Garrick or the Groucho. Stephen Fry wouldn't
get a look in; Lord Bragg would be shown the door before
you can say 'What, is *The South Bank Show* still on, then?'
To join a leek club you have to prove yourself worthy and
that means having your crop monitored by the membership committee for up to five years.

That the Vegetable and Produce Show was back, and
boasting a serious leek section, was a sign of the changing
nature of things. In the past decade, food has become a
middle class preoccupation, while gardening has begun to
achieve a trendiness unthinkable in the days when most
TV gardening shows were hosted by old blokes with hands
like gnarled roots and faces to match. Allotments – once
the exclusive preserve of World War II veterans armed
with greenfly sprayers and catapults for chasing off cats,
pigeons and small boys – are now being colonised by
urbane thirty-somethings who idolise Nigella Lawson and
Monty Don. Vegetable growing has started to attract an
audience that previously wouldn't have looked twice at a
leek unless it was in a bowl of chilled vichyssoise in 'a
little family-run place we know in the Dordogne'.
Suddenly, even the Oxford University website has advice
on how to grow blanch leeks using cardboard storage
tubes.

Mr Fudgie had joined the renascent Leek Club. 'It's
amazing really,' he said. 'We'd lived here for ten years and
hardly knew any locals, but since I got into the leeks I
can't step out the door without someone saying hello.'

The only worry about it all, as far as I could see, was
that the new breed of bourgeois grower wouldn't quite be
up to the rough and tumble of this, frankly, manly pursuit.

In leek-growing circles competition is fierce and at times unscrupulous. The recipes for success are a closely guarded secret. Some swear by brown ale, or dried ox-blood. Others mix up patented fertilisers with contents lists that read like the witches' speech in *Macbeth*. A dead dog in a water butt is not unheard of, nor is irrigating your leek-bed with the wife's wee (higher in nutrients than men's urine, apparently). And, cutting right against the grain of those seeking authentic organic produce, there are increasing whispers of Genetic Modification. Should prize vegetables take drug tests? As the white barrels of the leeks began to put on girth like a rogue bodybuilder, it was a question some were asking.

But, while the size of your Jumbo or Sammy Dickinson is important, it's not the only thing that counts among leek-growers. Leeks are also judged on physical perfection, with marks reduced for blemishes. As a result, everyone in the leek-growing fraternity has a tale of bitter rivals slashing leaves, or punching holes in them with airgun pellets. With such open warfare commonplace, there's little wonder leeks are grown in trenches.

And if your enemies don't get you nature might. A hungry field mouse or a boring eelworm can undo the work of months in a single minute. A few years ago, prize leeks in Felton near Morpeth were said to be menaced by a giant rabbit 'with one ear larger than the other'. With top prizes of £500 and the seeds from a champion speci-men selling for up to £20 a piece, there's no wonder some top growers spend the last week before a big show camped out in the garden to keep an eye on things.

The village Vegetable and Produce Show was a more modest and laid-back affair. Mr Fudgie said he would never get obsessive, even if it meant collecting the wooden spoon year on year. 'It's just a bit of fun, really, isn't it?' he said. 'Although obviously I'd be grateful if you didn't tell the lads at the leek club I said that.'

I told him his secret was safe with me.

When I had taken Manny out the previous evening the sky was clear and there was already ice on the windscreen of the car. Now, though, that had all gone and the day was grey and overcast. Sometimes it seemed that the weather along the Tyne Valley changed by the hour. When we first moved into the cottage the man who came to connect the electricity warned us about the erratic local climate. 'See,' he said, screwing down the metre, 'we're right in the middle of the country, halfway between the Atlantic and the North Sea, so we get the weather from two directions,' he tightened the final screw and stepped down from his ladder. 'Sometimes both at once.'

The one thing that can always be relied on is the wind. It blows remorselessly from the west, funnelled along the narrow valley. Some winds have names. There is the Harmattan of the Sahara, the Sirocco of the eastern Mediterranean, the Egyptian Khamsin, Australia's Southerly Buster, the Chinook in Colorado, the Mistral in the Rhone Valley, while way out west they have a name for the wind, the rain and the forest fire; the fire is Tess, the rain is Bess but they call the wind Maria. In the Sudan there is a wind named the Haboob, which is actually the Arab word for 'wind', a fact that suggests brand-management and advertising may not be a strong point in Khartoum. 'This is our latest design of car. We call it "The Car."' Still, at least the Sudanese had done better than the Northumbrians. Despite the fact that a westerly wind has been yodelling down the Tyne Valley for centuries, no one has bothered to christen it. I like to think of it as the Gilsland Up-Your-Jumper.

'It's what I call a lazy wind,' Mr Dodds said when I met him in the wood. 'Can't be bothered to go round you, so it just goes straight through.' Mr Dodds was standing with Taffy, watching the salmon swimming up the burn. There was an old mill race here that had originally been used to grind corn and had later been turned over to providing electricity for the big house. (There'd been a fashion for hydro-electricity in Northumberland in Victorian times, a fad inspired by the great Tyneside industrialist Lord Armstrong, who'd had hydroelectric turbines installed in his baronial manor at Rothbury.) The water for the race had been supplied via a small dam. The dam was now broken in the middle but the gap was three feet above the level of the stream up which the salmon were swimming and the water surged through it at quite a rate. The salmon approached the gap slowly, moving from side to side across the front of it as if testing the current or attempting to nerve themselves for the leap. Once they were ready they'd turn away in a slow arc and then swim at the gap as fast as they could before hurling themselves upwards. If they hit the torrent head on with sufficient power their streamlined shape meant they generally made it, but if they came in at even the slightest angle the water span them sideways and they were hurled straight back to where they had begun. Here they loitered for a while, trying to regain their energy for another attempt. One large fish tried four times while we were watching, each effort ending in failure.

'It seems an awful lot of hard work just to have bairns,' Mr Dodds said as we walked off up the burn. We bumped into Tommy and Tadger at the top of the wood. The little terrier came towards us in an unusually circumspect manner. No somersaults or flips this time. He came forward crab-fashion, quivering slightly and gazing up at me with imploring eyes, like a ham actor playing Smike.

'He's in disgrace,' Tommy said. What had happened was that Tommy's granddaughter had been given a Furby for her birthday and Tadger had rather taken a fancy to it. 'Whenever she leaves it on the floor I come in and find him on top of it, humping away,' Tommy said. 'I think he'd have got bored by now only the bloody thing makes that cooing noise when you squeeze it and he's taken that as a sign of encouragement. I'm just glad she didn't get one of those ones that lays an egg. Heaven knows what would come out of that if it hatched.'

'Hang on a minute,' I said. 'I thought he'd been neutered.'

'You know that, and I know that,' Tommy said, 'but he doesn't seem to have got the message.'

We had gone up to a colliery museum in east Northumberland with our friend Will, his children and their two dogs. Next to the colliery museum was what the local council dubbed a 'country park'. Wherever there has once been mining there is always a country park. It's either that or a dry ski slope. The country park was as flat as a plasterer's cap, the vast and forbidding plain broken by stands of pale, thin birch trees that seemed to be clustering together for safety. Gigantic electricity pylons towered above, the cables emitting a noise like the distant murmur of an angry mob. Despite the unsettling surroundings, an icy wind and the grim and glowering darkness of the sky, we decided we should all go for a walk.

We got the dogs out of the car, untangled their leads and tried to find correct rainwear for the children. There was the usual rigmarole of missing wellingtons, itchy hats, boots that rubbed and totally unsuitable coats. 'But you didn't tell me to bring a waterproof jacket,' somebody yelled. 'I didn't tell you to bring your head, but you didn't leave that behind,' another answered. A voice pointed out that since the head was attached to the body it was physically impossible to forget it; another bellowed, 'If we don't go soon it will be bloody dark.' And we untangled the dogs' leads again and headed off.

'Which way shall we go?' the children asked.

'I think,' Will said, casting around, 'we should go off that way.' He pointed to the east where a dozen windmills stood on a low knoll, pointing out towards the North Sea. It was hardly an inspiring vista but the only other choice involved walking towards a Harvester restaurant.

In many ways, wind turbines are the most modern-looking structures in the English countryside. The one thing that has actually materialised amid the personal hover-jets, suspended mono-rails and pill-sized meals of the *Eagle* comic's 'The World in the Space Age' features. They are the machines of tomorrow: white, clean and silent.

The Danes had been the first to really get into wind power. When we were on holiday one spring on Bornholm Island we met a retired Danish engineer with the amiable big-chinned face of a Moomin and he had told us how, even in the steam age, when the practice of harnessing the wind to power machinery fell into disuse across most of Europe, Denmark had remained faithful to the energy-generating windmill. During the Victorian era, when everyone else was burning fossil fuels like there was no tomorrow, the Danes marched against the tide, continuing to train 'wind electricians' and 'wind prospectors'. These latter were men whose job it was to test, using huge spruce poles, for areas where the raw resource was at its most abundant. Though they were actually sober technicians, it's hard not to hear the phrase without thinking of a grizzled old-timer – possibly played by Walter Brennan – in a union suit, or conjuring up images of what happened when he struck lucky and the cry went up of, 'There's wind in them thar hills,' inevitably sparking a mass wave of speculators to arrive in what historians would doubtless record as 'a windrush'.

A century and a half later and the world has, in some small way at least, come round to the Danish way of thinking. There are currently forty-two wind farms in Great Britain with a total of 748 operational turbines, in clusters ranging in size from a handful to a couple of dozen, generating enough electricity to meet the needs of 200,000 households. They are dotted around the nation from Antrim to Norfolk, the Highlands to Cornwall.

What is most striking about wind turbines is their almost total soundlessness. The swish of the vast rotor-blades chopping through the air is so slight that at distances of two hundred yards it is masked by the sound of the breeze rustling through the undergrowth. Modern techniques, such as the use of 'soft' gear-wheels, keep mechanical noise to a barely discernible minimum.

Yet there is something unnerving about this disproportional quiet. The human mind demands that a machine so big must have a concomitant racket. Maybe that is why there are unconfirmed reports that the turbines actually generate low-frequency sounds which, via some harmonic quirk, can be amplified by the exterior structure of certain homes into an irritating and persistent hum. Psychological damage to the inhabitants may, it is alleged, result. Perhaps this is not so surprising. After all, the thought that the pale, whirring giants who stalk a nearby hill are using your house as a loudspeaker would unsettle even the most firmly hinged citizen.

There is definitely a touch of sci-fi about the wind turbine, though I felt that it owed more to the bland dystopia envisaged by J. G. Ballard than the spiffing square-chinned heroics of Dan Dare.

By the time we got halfway to the turbines it had begun to rain. It wasn't ordinary rain, either. It was a wild and slanting rain that rattled off your anorak with a sound like automatic fire. It was an unstoppable and dense rain. Within five minutes I realised that not only were my jeans wet through, my underpants were too. My boots were waterproof, but that hardly mattered since water was running down my legs and forming puddles in them.

The weather and the surroundings had subdued the dogs. It was so appalling even the children had ceased to complain. Will told uplifting stories about the horrors of his days at a prep school in a bid the cheer them up. He said that it had been very cold at his school and so he had written to his mother requesting some gloves. His handwriting was very poor, however, and when the parcel arrived from home it contained not gloves but a packet of cloves. Later Will challenged his mother on the topic. 'Why on earth did you think a seven-year-old boy would want cloves?' he said.

'Well,' his mother replied, 'it was December and I thought perhaps you were going to stick them in an orange and make Christmas punch.'

Will said that at weekends he would be taken to visit an

aunt. The aunt believed that what boys needed was a good blast of fresh air and she insisted on taking him for a hike no matter how bad the weather was. A few years ago, he said, he had come across his old diary from that time and one entry had read simply: 'Sunday. Another foul walk with Aunt Mary.'

'And now,' Will said to the children as the car park at last came into view again, 'when you get home you can all write something similar in yours.'

November

'You might want to get yon fella on his lead,' Mr Dodds said when I bumped into him at the point in the riverside path where the birch and rowan trees stand so close to the water's edge that their lower branches are permanently thatched with flood debris. Usually it's just twigs, straw, shredded bale-bags and plastic bottles, but once there had been a brand new yellow leather football and another time a voluminous sage-green brassiere. You could only speculate on what the story behind *its* journey was.

Mr Dodds held his nose between his thumb and fore-finger and indicated Taffy. 'Little beggar,' he said. Taffy looked up at me.

Our West Highland, Doogie, loved to roll in anything fruity. Usually the evidence of his visit to Mother Nature's perfume counter was plain to see on his white fur, but even when it wasn't you knew what he'd been up to by his manner. After he'd applied a noxious coating to himself Doogie strutted toward you, stiff legged, tail high, eyes bright, exuding the testosterone-fuelled smugness of a man walking into a pub the night after bedding the Pussycat Dolls.

Taffy wore that same expression. If he could have whistled a merry tune he would have done.

November is a bad time to walk a dog along the banks of a salmon river. The salmon are coming upstream to spawn. Exhausted by the effort, starving through sexual frenzy they fall prey to *Gyrodactylus salaris*, a tiny parasite that affects their skin, gills and fins. The parasite could be carried on fishing gear and boats. There were posters all along the riverbank warning fishermen and canoeists to keep their equipment clean. That didn't stop it spreading, though. Dozens of sick fish loitered in the shallows, motionless and gasping, their skin mottled and shredded. They were ugly and mutant, the sort of thing you'd expect to bang pitifully on the bunker door during a nuclear winter.

Eventually, a rise in the water-level deposited the fish on land and they stuck there, decomposing and filling the air with a stench so powerful it seemed to hover in the air like a cloud of midges. Unfortunately this sort of odour has the same effect on dogs as the Sirens' song had on Greek sailors. Dogs will rub their heads and necks in anything that stinks. If dogs ran The Body Shop you'd be washing yourself in fox-dung shower gel and burning badger-scat scented candles. To dogs rotting fish is the ultimate grooming product.

'Why do they do it?' I asked Mr Dodds when I'd secured Manny. Mr Dodds had worked with dogs all his life. Taffy's father Dewi had herded cattle, nipping at their heels like Nobby Stiles pursuing Antonio Rattin across the field at Wembley.

'Camouflage,' Mr Dodds said wisely. 'If they were in the wild, approaching a herd of deer, the deer would smell that,' he wafted a hand at Taffy, 'and they wouldn't reckon it was the scent of a predator.'

It seemed reasonable enough. Deer are sensitive to smell. Keith the gamekeeper told me that if he was working in the woods with a chainsaw, or loading up the pheasant feeders, the deer paid him no attention. But if he had his gun and was hunting something they ran off as soon as they saw him. At first he thought it was the shape of the gun that alarmed them. 'Then, one time, I'd had a row with somebody,' he says. 'I went up in the wood after and I was still steaming. Didn't have the gun, but the deer belted away when they saw me coming, as if I had.' He thinks they scented adrenalin.

That dogs would adopt an olfactory disguise to cover their aggressive intent appeared plausible. When I was walking home, however, a thought occurred to me. I imagined the deer feeding and the dog approaching. One deer saying to the other 'What's that?' and the other sniffing the air and saying, 'Don't worry it's only a fish. And (sniff, sniff), if I'm not mistaken, it's been deceased for at least a week and a half.' And the first deer saying, 'Well, can I just remark that for a dead fish it's running bloody fast . . . argh!'

A few months later two deer would meet up in a forest glade and during a chat one would say to the other, 'Now tell me, what ever happened to your friend Bernard?' And the second deer would shake his antlers sadly and say, 'Terrible tragedy. Eaten, I'm sorry to say . . . by a dead fish.' And the first deer would say, 'Gosh, it's amazing how often that happens, isn't it?'

Somewhere in the murk of the morning I could see flashing lights moving a foot or so above the dark ground. Every once in a while they stopped momentarily and then moved on again. For a lot of my life I have been scared of seeing a UFO. It's not that I fear alien abduction, you understand, it's just that I'm genuinely terrified of becoming one of those people who say, 'Well, I was sceptical too, myself, but then one day . . .' and conclude '. . . and there's just no other logical explanation for it.' There's nothing more pathetic than a converted cynic.

Luckily it soon became apparent that what I was witnessing was not a visitation from a far-off galaxy but Tommy's dog wearing a light-up collar. '£3.75 from the pet shop. A right bargain,' Tommy said. He said that in the winter Tadger was always getting lost. He ran off after a pheasant or rabbit and Tommy and his wife had no idea where he'd gone. 'Now he's got this thing on we always know where he is,' he said.

Tommy said that the previous day his wife had been down in the town walking Tadge in the riverside park. He'd disappeared off and she'd been calling and calling for him. Then from over the other side of the golf course she'd heard a male voice bellowing back, 'He's ow-er here, pet, and I think he's been to a disco.'

Tommy was a man who collected wild food. Not in any sort of fanatical way, I should say. Though I'd read that in medieval times they used to put the freshly sprouted hawthorn leaves into salads and flavour junket with cowslips, that wasn't the sort of thing Tommy went in for – he was a countryman, not a crank. Crab apples, blackberries, bullaces, wild cherries, hazelnuts, rowans and bilberries were more his line. He was particularly good on field mushrooms, regularly leaving a large bag of them on our doorstep first thing in the morning. He was happy to give them away, but he was very reluctant to reveal where he actually got them. If you asked him where he picked his mushrooms he'd gesture vaguely in the direction of

Hadrian's Wall and name a string of improbable-sounding geographical features full of arcane Northumbrian pronunciations: 'Up beyond Blackcockhaugh, just where Shieldinglough meets Poltrosscleugh. If you get to Wifey Waugh's Sike you've gone too far.' Part of me thought he was making them up just to confuse people.

One frosty morning, I bumped into Tommy and Tadger in the cut that ran down into the Burn Wood. The cut was flanked by two crumbling stone walls, eight feet high, that suggested the narrow muddy lane had once been of some importance. Growing along the south-facing wall were a couple of large blackthorns. Tommy had a carrier bag in his hand. He was surveying the bushes and shaking his head.

When I greeted him he said, 'I can't figure this out. The last time I looked, ten days back, these were covered in berries and now they've all gone.'

'Well, hasn't someone else just come along before you?' I suggested.

'No,' Tommy said. 'Anybody who picks sloes knows you have to wait until after the first frost or they're no good. The skin's too hard. Today's the first frost and no one else could have been here before me because there are no foot-marks.'

I'd heard this before about sloes – that the frost made the tough hide more permeable. Otherwise they were rock hard and strangely reluctant to give up their acidic juice. Tommy said he was going to flavour gin with them. He made a batch every year, then left it for twelve months to mature. He said that after they'd been soaking in gin for that long even the sour sloe berries became quite palatable. 'Nice with a bit of ice cream and a ginger snap,' he said, smacking his lips.

As he was saying this a thought struck me. 'You don't suppose,' I said, 'that somebody could have come and picked them last week and then bunged them in the freezer for a few hours do you?'

Tommy looked at me for a moment as his mind absorbed what I had just said, then he slapped his hand to his forehead, 'Way, bugger me.'

To look north-eastwards from Walltown Crags is to gaze upon an English wilderness. The grey-green rocks of the Whin Sill drop down seventy feet to a cork-coloured plain that stretches into the distance, its surface broken by scattered patches of maroon heather and the occasional pockmark of glistening black groundwater. What few trees that survive are small and twisted, hunchbacked against the prevailing westerly wind that rattles the bent grass and sends the cawing jackdaw frantically tumbling across an ashen sky. An eighteenth-century Scottish writer would cast his eyes across this empty waste and sardonically note: 'It is a comfortless piece of way for the traveller.' An ideal place then, all in all, for a walk with Little Man.

On a freezing mid-November morning in Brocolitia car park at Hadrian's Wall there were visitors from Yokohama, The Hague and Oklahoma. They winced from the lash of the wind as they changed into stout waterproof footwear and prepared to walk across the sludgy ground to the ruins of a small temple, where soldiers of the Roman Empire from Belgium, Romania and Syria once offered sacrifices to the Persian sun god, Mithras.

Nowadays, Hadrian's Wall is a UNESCO World Heritage Site. It wasn't always so highly regarded. Until Victorian times, stone from the wall was routinely pilfered. Whole sections were summarily dismantled and the immaculately cut masonry was turned into farms, barns and dwellings. During the reign of Henry VIII, Lord Dacre took apart an entire fort at Drumburgh and had it made into a 'pretty pyle' of a castle for himself. The greatest damage of all was done in 1746 when General Wade, anxious to move troops from Newcastle into Dumfriesshire in the aftermath of the Jacobite Rebellion, built a highway – still called the Military Road – using the wall as his hard core.

As a consequence of these ravages, Hadrian's barrier against barbarism is now rarely more than six feet high, and usually much less than that. What once kept out the most determined woad-painted invaders is now barely proof against the odd lethargic school party.

But if it is low in stature it is rich in atmosphere. Stand in the soggy trough of land near the Brocolitia temple Mithraeum (a plateau scoured almost featureless by the abrasive gale, with the purple mass of the Pennines looming to the south and to the north, nothing) and you soon feel as our ancestors must once have done – small in a big world.

Manny and I walked down from Brocolitia fort on a straight footpath that came out just above the church field in our village. I had seen the footpath many times when Ingo was alive and always thought, 'One day, we'll go up there.' It had taken fifteen years to get around to it. 'Who knows,' I said to Manny as we set off across the brown and springy ground, 'at this rate I could be re-puttying that pantry window by 2012.'

We soon entered a flat upland of bob cotton, reeds and tussocky knolls. The ground was uneven and it was plain that nobody had walked the footpath for, well, fifteen years, in all probability. It was hard going. The long spiky grass meant Manny had to bounce along and I kept losing

my footing. Larks flew up as we approached and a herd of
brindled bullocks watched our unsteady progress with
mild curiosity.

As we crossed a shallow stream-bed, a hare jumped up
in front of us and sped off, skimming lightly over the
rough surface of the land. Ingo had once put up a hare in
a newly mowed meadow near Haughton Castle on the
North Tyne. The hare had started off at a lazy pace, as if
disturbed from an afternoon nap, but the minute the dog
got to within a few yards it suddenly kicked out its back
legs and zoomed off, smoothly accelerating to maximum
speed as though it was running up through the gears
before finally switching on the turbocharger. Ingemar was
not easily discouraged when in pursuit of something. He
had once chased two roe deer across a vast field filled with
rapeseed. As they bobbed elegantly through the high
plants, a flash of white bottoms among the yellow flowers,
Ingo flailed away in their wake. Even though we couldn't
see him he was easily tracked by following the thrashing
noise and the frantic waving of the plants. He carried on
for four hundred yards like this, abandoning only when
the deer leapt effortlessly over a five-foot wall and disappeared among some Scots pines. But he followed the hare
for only twenty yards before pulling to a halt. Even Ingo
recognised that he was totally outclassed.

I wasn't sure Manny would have given up, however.
Hares stick to their territory, which covers about two
square miles, so any pursuer who has the stamina and the
stubbornness to follow them round and round in circles
for long enough will eventually wear them down.
Stubbornness and stamina, along with a good nose, were
the PBGV's big strengths. I was glad I had him on the
lead.

It was fitting that the hare should live near the wall: it was the Romans that had introduced the brown hare into Britain. I sometimes wondered what animals there would actually have been in this country if we hadn't been invaded so often during our formative years. The Romans brought hares, pheasants and dormice, the Normans brought rabbits, and later on came red-legged partridges, fallow deer, black rats, brown rats and the house mouse. Of course, while these animals were being introduced, the same people who were carefully importing them were also busy wiping out indigenous wildlife such as wild short-horned cattle, wolves, beaver, aurochs, brown bear and wild boar.

We plunged on through the heavy grass. By now the sky had darkened and the icy wind was whipping itself into a righteous froth. Soon rain the texture of cuckoo spit was lashing our right flank, plastering Manny's fur to his body so that he looked like a teenage boy who'd overdone the hair gel. It was another hour before we arrived at the foot-path sign in the village.

By the time we got home, the whole of the west-facing side of my body was as numb as a gatepost. I was thinking of the wax tablet in the Vindolanda museum. Sent to a Roman soldier based on the wall 1700 years ago, it reads, 'I have sent two pairs of socks from Sattua, two pairs of sandals and two pairs of underpants'. In his patrols along the wall the recipient must have been sorely tempted to wear both pairs of the latter simultaneously.

Big cylindrical hay bales were piled up in the corner of the field. As we drew nearer I could see dozens of brown rats scurrying along the tops of them and disappearing inside. Manny doesn't show much interest in rats, which is a relief in some respects. Ingemar had been quite an expert with them. According to what source you believed, standard schnauzers had either been cart, or carriage dogs. Either way, one of their duties had been to keep stables free of rodents. When Ingo was excited he had a habit of pounding the ground with his front paws: bang, bang, bang, like a boxer hitting a punch bag. It was part of the instinct that had been isolated in schnauzers by years of breeding. When Ingo went after a rat, he didn't scoop it up with his mouth and shake it as a terrier would have done, he simply bashed it over the head. It was lethally effective and frankly I was very pleased whenever he did it. Except that after he'd killed one he invariably picked up the quivering body in his jaws and brought it to me as a gift. It was a nice thought but, as Mrs Pelham-Beale said one morning when she came across us just after Ingo had emerged from round the back of the bales, a limp naked tail drooping down one side of his beard, 'There is something about a dog with a dead rat in his mouth that rather puts one off one's porridge.'

There are people who like rats, and they will tell you that they are intelligent, affectionate and very hygienic. I would like to believe that, but I can't. Instead when I think of rats I think of a description of the brown rat written by the naturalist A. W. Rees: 'There is no courtesy or kindness in his nature. He is a cannibal – even the young and sick of his own kind become the victims of his rapacious hunger – and he will eat anything, living or dead, from the refuse in the garbage heap to the dainty egg of a willow-wren in the tiny doomed nest amid the briars at the margin of the river.'

You see, at one time all the buildings around our cottage had been barns and byres. Gradually, though, they had all been converted into houses. Suddenly the rats, which for years had been happily spending the winter in the barns, had nowhere to go and so they decided to take up residence in our sheds instead. One night, when I was washing up at the kitchen sink that looked out on the back garden, I counted eleven of them scurrying about in the moonlight.

And when the sheds got a bit chilly the rats discovered a corner of our house where the pointing had crumbled away, got inside the stone wall and gradually worked their way upwards. One night Catherine and I heard the noise of something running about in the ceiling void above our bedroom. 'That's just a mouse, isn't it?' I said hopefully. 'I mean, it sounds much larger than it really is because it's hollow up there.'

Pitter-patter, pitter-patter, went the feet above our heads. They stopped. Then we heard a ripping noise. 'It's eating the insulation,' Catherine said.

'I don't understand that,' I said. 'How can they stand to do it? If you get any on your skin it itches for weeks. What must it be like when it's in your stomach? And it must be very painful when it comes out the other end.'

We listened to the noise. 'I don't think it's a mouse,' Catherine said. 'It doesn't move around fast enough.' I knew she was right, because earlier in the week I had put a mousetrap up in the loft without telling her. I had heard it go off when I was working one afternoon, but when I went up to empty it I couldn't find it anywhere. Whatever it had caught had walked off with the trap still attached. That didn't seem like the work of a field mouse to me.

'It couldn't fall through on our heads, could it?' Catherine asked as the ripping sound continued. I assured her that it couldn't because the ceiling was solid pine and firmly screwed onto the beams. But I stayed awake all night just in case, and the next morning I phoned the rodent exterminator.

He arrived two days later in a white van with a sign on the side that proclaimed his profession so loudly I couldn't understand why he hadn't gone the whole hog and painted up his 'kills' on the bonnet like a fighter pilot.

The rodent man was small and active. He talked me through the habits of rats and outlined his plans for tackling ours rather in the manner, I imagine, Jim Corbett must have explained to the local Government Commissioner how he was going to deal with a man-eating Bengal tiger. 'Several runs identified in and around sheds one, two and three,' he said, 'with a clear indication of activity in the vicinity of the south-western corner of the property.'

The rodent exterminator said the rat population was getting out of control. It was a boom time for them. Milder winters were one factor and then there was the change in human eating-habits. 'People these days chuck out their leftovers,' he said. 'It's not like when we were kids and you never got a meal that didn't have a bit of yesterday's dinner in it, is it?' he said.

'They say that today in Britain you are never more than twelve feet from a rat,' the rodent exterminator said as he surveyed the house. He glanced up at our bedroom ceiling. 'Still, for you, twelve feet would be a bit of an improvement at the moment.'

As Manny and I walked along the burn a heron took off, lumbering up into the air with its characteristic pterodactyl-like squawking. Dylan Thomas thought that herons looked like priests. I'm not so sure. To me, they have a solitary, lugubrious and slightly seedy air. There is something furtive about them. They are always alone, lurking, their wings pulled around them like raincoats. They put me in mind of the sort of men who might hide in the shrubbery and expose themselves to passing women.

Admittedly, the low esteem in which I hold them has been exacerbated by an incident when Maisie was four. We'd been walking along the river with a friend of hers one day when we saw a female mallard being trailed by a flock of fluffy ducklings. The ducklings were squeaking and struggling to keep up, wings flapping, beaks opening and closing with effort. As they passed us I noticed a heron standing in the water. It appeared to be paying no attention to the mallard family, ignoring the mother duck as she swept past, but when her offspring came into range it lunged once, twice, three times, catching a duckling each time and swallowing it whole with a toss of its head.

The two little girls had watched this scene. I'd thought they would be shocked, but Maisie's friend simply shrugged and said, 'It's the circle of life, isn't it? Like in *The Lion King*?' The two of them started singing the theme from the Disney film and soon forgot all about it. Sometimes you have to be grateful for Elton John.

At the stile through into the pine plantation we met Mr Fudgie. He said it had been a rough few days. Mr Fudgie said that his wife was in a terribly bad mood. She had been worried about her weight for many years, Mr Fudgie said, and as such was very sensitive about it. 'The other day the next-door neighbour asked if we could look after her baby for the morning,' Mr Fudgie said. 'A right little poppet, she is. So the wife and I took her out for a walk in the pram. Some old biddy from the old people's bungalows is walking along towards us and when she gets to us we

stop. And she's looking at the baby and cooing and twittering and what have you. She says, "Oh, what a lovely
child," and then she looks up at the wife, glances down at
her stomach and says, "And another one of the way, I see."
Then she says cheerio and buggers off. The wife's been
stood in front of the mirror ever since. And that was three
days back.'

Mr Fudgie said that the last time he had seen his wife
this upset was after the business in the greengrocers. He
said he'd gone in with his wife and she'd asked the man
behind the counter for five pounds of small onions. The
greengrocer had said, 'Are you pickling?' and Mr Fudgie
had said, 'No, it's just the rain running off her mac.' Mrs
Fudgie had said she had never been so embarrassed in all
her born days and had not spoken to him for nearly a
week.

While Mr Fudgie and I were talking a lad walked past
with a white bull terrier on a rope lead. The lad had so
many tattoos he really ought to have come in two vol-
umes. The dog didn't have any tattoos but rather looked
as if it ought to. Mr Fudgie waved to the lad, who waved
back in a desultory manner. Mr Fudgie chuckled. The lad
had worked for the same firm as him for a while and
looked a lot harder than he actually was, he said. 'He
wants everyone to think he's a villain, but he's a nice
enough lad, all round,' he said, 'only he's a bit dozy.'

Mr Fudgie said that during the 2006 World Cup he'd
met the lad on the train to Newcastle. 'It was the day
England played Portugal in the quarter-finals, right? And
I was off to watch it with a load of mates of mine in
Prudhoe,' Mr Fudgie said. 'Now, on the morning of the
game it was the school fete and the wife was running the
face-painting stall with our Katie. So, just for a laugh, I got

them to do my face with the cross of St George. Then I
went home, put on my England shirt, picked up a case of
lager and went and got the train. So I'm sat there on the
train and that lad gets on. He sees me and he comes and
sits opposite. I'm sat there with the cross of St George
painted on my face, my England shirt on and case of beer
tucked under my arm on the day England are playing in
the World Cup quarter-final and the lad looks at me and
he says, "Off into town to do a bit of shopping, are you?"'

Mr Fudgie said that he'd told a workmate this story
and the bloke had said that that sounded just like the dozy
lad. He said the lad lived at home with his mother. He said
that one Saturday his mother had left the house, and on
the way down the street she'd seen a TV licence detector
van and a man getting out of it. She thought the man
might be looking for her because she'd let her licence lapse
and only just renewed it a few days before. So she went up
to the TV licence man and asked if it was number twenty-
two he'd come for.

The man had said that was correct. So the mother said
that she was the occupant but she was in a rush to get to
work and if he went to the house her son was in: 'Tell him
the licence is in the right-hand drawer of the kitchen
table.'

The man went to the house and knocked at the door.
The dozy lad answered. 'I need to see your TV licence,'
the man said.

'I don't know where it is,' the lad replied.

'It's in the right-hand drawer of the kitchen table,' the
man said.

'Blimey,' the lad said. 'Those TV licence detector vans
must be a lot more powerful than people think.'

*

I had to alter my normal route that lunchtime because the hunt was out and the hunt was something I generally tried to avoid getting tangled up with. Like many people who have grown up in the countryside, I am more or less ambivalent about the cruelty or otherwise of the enterprise. Indeed, since my own dogs had, over the years, killed dozens of rabbits, pheasants and rats I didn't feel I was in any position to take the moral high ground.

The reason I didn't like the hunt was because the people who followed it were so stuffed full of their own importance it was a wonder none of them had burst. And it had to be said that the government ban on hunting with dogs had only increased this monumental level of self-regard. The hunt followers now saw themselves as freedom fighters and as a consequence pomposity levels had reached such heights they were in danger of poking a hole in the ozone layer. This meant that going out for a walk with a dog when the hunt was on was to risk life and limb because everyone involved with the hunt was now under the impression they were in a war with the government and thus normal rules of conduct did not apply to them. On hunt day the narrow lanes were filled with mighty Japanese four-wheel drives. They surged around at improbable speeds showering you with mud and gravel and disappearing before you could yell, 'I see you've got an "I Slow Down For Horses" sticker in your rear window. How about slowing down for people too you selfish bastard?'

The late Brigadier Pelham-Beale (ret.) had been a well-known local sportsman. When I heard this I had briefly imagined him playing tennis, rugby, cricket or, possibly, racing sports cars on the banked track of Brooklands Raceway. In fact, it turned out that the Brigadier (ret.) was not so much a sportsman as a sporting man.

There is a great difference between sport and sporting, as anyone who has visited a second-hand bookshop will know. In a second-hand bookshop the sports section features mildewed old autobiographies by 1950s British footballers, who beam from the flyleaf, all Brylcreem and ration-book teeth, and touchingly declare their ambition 'to win the European Cup with Preston North End' and 1970s novels by Terry Venables in which he declares confidently that by the year 2000 all soccer will be played on Astroturf and the USA will be the dominant power in the world game.

The sporting books section, by contrast, carries works of an altogether heftier stamp, bound in embossed Edwardian rhino-hide and aimed at what the author's introductory blurb describes as 'country gentlemen and the modern gamekeeper'. Since gamekeepers are a breed whose idea of a sophisticated public relations campaign is to hang a row of dead stoats on a barbed wire fence, I should say this element represents a very small target audience. In fact, if it came to a free-for-all, I'd back dodos to swiftly overwhelm modern gamekeepers by sheer weight of numbers.

Sporting books generally have titles like *Every Boy's Guide to Mole Coursing*, *Colonel Bassoon-Binder's Quail Baiting Year* and *With Rod and Gun in the Rockies* by A. Chuffley-Plum Esq. (author of *Have Fun with Howitzers* and *A Taxidermist in the Chutt*). Occasionally a title such as *Everyman's Small Bore Shooting* catches the eye – though on closer inspection the volume proves, disappointingly, to be about firing a rifle at a target rather than, as you had anticipated, loosing off a few rounds from a .38 in the direction of Tom Cruise.

Those sporting books that are not devoted to killing things are about horse racing. I have a strong aversion to horse racing. Or rather I have a strong aversion to racehorses.

Years of aristocratic inbreeding have given the racehorse an innate sense of superiority. The race card tells us these glossy steeds are called Peasholme Lass or Windfall Warrior but I sense that the horses prefer to think of themselves as Hugo and Jemima.

Watching them in the parade ring before a major race, punters like to speculate on what they might be thinking. They imagine the horses are dreaming of speed and glory. In fact, they are worrying about the problems of finding a suitable nanny for young Toby, or trying to decide whether to sell the Freelander and get a Range Rover instead. That is, of course, if they are thinking anything at all. Horse-lovers constantly assure us that equines are frightfully clever, but ask yourself this: how intelligent can any animal be if a five-foot-high bloke who wears wellies twenty-four hours a day can train it?

Brigadier Pelham-Beale (ret.) had been fond of both horses and killing things. He'd also loved pugs. One in particular: a dog named Beaufort. Beaufort had not, as you might have surmised, been named after the famous hunt, but after the British admiral Sir Francis Beaufort, who invented the Beaufort scale for quantifying wind speeds. (The numbers correspond to the amount of sail a man-of-war could carry in such a wind.) Beaufort the pug had lived to a ripe old age. He was feisty and tough and had once 'had words' with an English mastiff. 'A real battling bantam,' Brigadier Pelham-Beale (ret.) had said, referring to the regiments of undersized soldiers who had fought in the frontline in World War I. In the last few years of his life Beaufort's bowed little legs barely had sufficient spring left in them to carry him, so on walks the Brigadier (ret.) had usually picked him up and tucked him under his arm.

'I think that on occasion my husband may have held that dog a little too tightly,' Mrs Pelham-Beale said, 'because when I came to empty his wardrobe some years after he passed away I found fossilised deposits in the pockets of several of his overcoats.' Her late husband, Mrs Pelham-Beale said, was not a man to stand around with his hands in his pockets, which, on balance, she concluded, was probably just as well.

December

From the high cliffs near the ruin of Staward Pele, where local freebooter Dickie of Kingswood once made his camp, you look out northwards across the steep cut of Northumberland's Allen Valley. Oak and ash forest fills the whole of your field of vision. In summer there are blue-bells, wild violets and pansies, ramblers, picnickers and the yells of children paddling in the shallow river, but on a midweek morning in winter it is a place of calm, austere beauty that no middle-aged man can look upon without a twinge of regret. For the seasons march on, and so much of our lives are wasted that might better have been spent perfecting a Johnny Weissmuller yell.

The cold aside, you can't help feeling that Tarzan would have been at home here, and not only because Greystoke is just a short elephant ride across the hills to the west. Staward Pele stands on the northern fringe of the area naturalist David Bellamy has dubbed 'England's Last Wilderness'. Since that title is also claimed by Exmoor in Devon, the National Parks Department have opted for the more prosaic (and longwinded) title of North Pennines Area of Outstanding Natural Beauty. Whatever you call it, the region that gives birth to the north-east's three great rivers – the Tees, the Wear and one half of the Tyne – is as close as England comes to untrammelled territory. Man has left his mark here, of course. This was once the richest source of lead in Britain. Though long since gone, there is evidence of the trade everywhere, in the old workings that cut the hillsides and the tall brick flues up which, so local tradition has it, small boys were sent once a year to crack off the silver that had adhered to the chimney sides. There are isolated clumps of trees, stunted and withered by the run-off, and Nonconformist chapels littering the valleys. Wherever there was mineral extraction there was Methodism. Now the mining has stopped and the Wesleyans, too, have suffered a downturn in their fortunes. The Temperance Hotels that were once a feature of the North Pennines have nearly all closed down and many of the chapels have been sold for houses; the current occupants battle not with drink and the devil but with the problem of how best to curtain arched windows. It would be easy to turn nostalgic, but lead mining was hardly the stuff of warm memories. It was grim and dirty, poor and poisonous. During the peak of the industry in the Allen Valley average male life expectancy dropped below thirty. Suicide was common. But if it is not quite virgin country then it is certainly chaste.

Little Man and I walked through the quiet woods. Beech leaves the colour of goldfish decorated the ground. There were said to be dormice – the most northerly colony – in the woods here. I looked about vaguely in the hope of seeing one, though I guessed there was little chance. As a boy the dormouse had been one of my favourite animals. I had read whole books devoted to them and every time we went to the south of England I searched desperately for them in the hope of capturing one and keeping it as a pet. Nowadays, however, there were only two things I could remember about the dormouse: that the Romans ate them and that they were said to be immune to the poison of the adder.

I watched Manny cock his leg on a fallen silver birch trunk. Little Man was very restrained when it came to leg cocking. For most dogs I had known leg cocking was grand ceremony that involved sniffing, circling, strutting, peeing and then scuffing and growling. Manny hardly bothered with any of that. Nor did he seem particularly concerned about marking his territory. Quite often he would only cock his leg half a dozen times during an entire walk. Doogie would have managed that in a stroll to the front gate and Ingemar was even worse. The road past our house ran down to a bridge. It is a distance of about a hundred yards. One morning when I took Ingo out I counted how often he cocked his leg between our drive and the bridge. The answer was twenty-eight times. No wonder I was never back in time for breakfast. Sometimes I had to cock my own leg, so to speak. When I did, Ingo would stand and look at me with bewilderment. 'What are you doing wasting it all in one spot?' he seemed to be saying. 'You could have ringed the whole village with that lot.'

Nor did Manny seem bothered about height. Most male dogs were obsessed with hitting the uppermost point they possibly could. Doogie would lift his leg so high and tilt back so far I felt sure one day he'd topple over and end up sending a stream of urine flying over his own head like a baby boy. I had seen many small dogs doing the same. They did it in an attempt to convince other males that they were bigger than they actually were. 'This territory belongs to Towser,' the pee mark said, 'and before you mess with his patch, just take a look how tall he is.'

At some point in the autumn, when the fire is lit and rain is beating out a semaphore signal on the roof (the message reads: 'Why didn't you unblock the drains while you had the chance, you lazy bugger?') Catherine will ask, 'What would *you* like to do at Christmas?' This is a hard one to answer. Easier by far to say what I don't want to do.

Like most men – and dogs – I can't abide fuss. Fuss upsets the delicate yin and yang of my universe, it unbalances my natural equilibrium and, what's more, it makes washing-up. This is why men invented Pot Noodle.

Fatherhood has altered my attitude to washing-up. (In a house full of children, where else but in front of a frothing sink can a man find the peace he needs to contemplate the big questions. Is advancement the same as progress? Are faith and science irreconcilable? How did the theme from *Top Cat* go?) My attitude to fuss remains the same, however. And at no time in the year is fuss and all the collateral damage to the male psyche that it entails more guaranteed than at Christmas. The festive season is a week-long tidal wave of turmoil.

Of course, there are many things a man might do to limit the upheaval. He might, for instance, tell his children that the television is broken beyond repair in early October thus avoiding constantly having to hear about 'this cool new action toy that was just advertised and, like, it looks like a rocket, right? But with two twists it turns into this mega-mechanoid-robot-lizard that squirts poisonous lava from its neck cavity'. He might respond to his daughter's tales of the latest doll that is 'just like a real baby girl' by saying, 'What, you mean she crawls into the kitchen

and eats from the dog's dinner bowl?' and, most effec-
tively, he might banish all talk of a Traditional Family
Christmas from his house from now until the end of eter-
nity. Or at least until the football has finished.

Naturally enough, he will not do any of these things. To
do so would bring him into conflict with his loved ones.
Children love a Traditional Family Christmas because
they are showered with gifts and allowed to eat sherbet
flying-saucers for breakfast. And women love a Traditional
Family Christmas because, well, when it comes to pain
they have selective memories. That is how they are able to
have more than one baby. And if they can forget the
agony of childbirth how can we expect them to remember
that Christmas trees drop needles all over the floor that
stick in your socks?

I have seen it all before, as a boy. As yuletide
approached and the question of what we were going to
do arose, my father would say, 'I think these days we
have forgotten the true meaning of Christmas, which is,
of course, to spread the maximum of misery over the greatest possible distance. I therefore vote that we invite the
family round.'

My mother was immune to his sarcasm, though in fairness to my father it should be said he was speaking largely
in her interests.

My mother would spend the whole of Christmas Day
in the kitchen. By 7 a.m. it was so filled with steam and
smoke it resembled a foggy night on Exmoor. Shadowy
figures moved about in the smog. These were my mother's
aunts – all six of them. They had arrived an hour earlier
because they held the old-fashioned British view that if
you wanted vegetables to be ready for lunchtime you had
to begin boiling them at dawn. In my great-aunts' world a

cabbage wasn't properly done until it was a formless sludge. To this day I can't see a beached jellyfish without thinking of Aunty Bertha's Brussels sprouts.

At nine o'clock my grandmother would arrive. 'I better get in that kitchen and make myself useful,' she'd say. My grandmother's idea of making herself useful in the kitchen was to sit in the corner drinking Emva Cream and offering advice. She had perfected the art of backseat cooking. 'You go ahead, honey, don't mind me,' Granny would say. 'Though, if it was my choice, I'd put it in a bigger dish.'

The worst was yet to come, however. Because shortly before noon my grandfather's sisters, Ethel and Edna, would arrive from the East Cleveland hills and with them came a whiff of gin and brimstone, and their mongrel Scamp.

Scamp was a deeply unprepossessing dog. His bony hide was the colour of slurry, his hair so smooth he was, to all intents and purposes, bald. He had sharp teeth, a thin, drooping tail and entered a room with the meek and cowed demeanour of Uriah Heep approaching the nobility. Like Dickens' character, he was filled with low cunning. He snatched rusks from the hands of babes and cocked his leg on the clothes-horse when no one was looking.

Scamp was so unprepossessing, in fact, that once, when Ethel and Edna were out walking him on his lead (a length of old washing line – they couldn't abide waste), a youth remarked loudly: 'How look, yon biddies have got a rat on a rope.' And the Rat on a Rope was what everyone else in the family called him ever after.

Despite this, there was a distinct Garbo-esque quality about the dog. It is said that when the great Swedish actress entered a room no man could take his eyes off her. The same was true of Scamp. Though this had less to do with his radiance and more with the fact that if you turned away from him for even a split second he was likely to savage your calves.

The attacks were only ever against men. With women and girls Scamp was all oily charm. He wagged his slender tail. He smiled winsomely. He lapped sweet sherry from the palms of their hands, then turned tipsy somersaults at their feet. But with men it was a different matter. Too cunning to risk an all-out frontal assault, Scamp bided his time and mastered the art of the ambush. Many fellows with military experience attempted to outwit him down the years but failed. Scamp was unstoppable. Though experience taught that a couple of copies of the *Radio Times* stuck down the back of your socks would at least limit the pain.

Why Scamp hated men so much is hard to say. The aunts were charitable women – or at least they liked things that were free – and had got him from the local dogs' home. (What criteria they used to pick him they never said, though most of those who knew the animal were forced to conclude that they had simply walked in and asked the person behind the desk for something little and vicious.) Perhaps he had been brutally treated by a male owner. Or maybe it was just the spirit of the age. It was the seventies. Women were angry. So was Scamp.

Like Frederick the Weimeraner's owner, the aunts could see no ill in their pet. Ethel and Edna could always find a reasonable explanation for even the most psychotic of Scamp's acts.

On one particularly noteworthy occasion the dog attacked the man who had come to read the gas meter.

The gas man was well known locally. A blameless little chap, he had suffered a hideous childhood trauma. His mother had been the cook for a retired Guards officer of ancient lineage. This gentleman, a bachelor, took what would now doubtless be regarded as a suspicious interest in the physical well-being of his servants' male children, but it was then thought of as benevolent paternalism – even when it involved nude bathing.

Seeing that the boy was below average height, the master had approached the local GP and asked if it mightn't be possible to 'stretch him a trifle'. When the doctor rebuffed the suggestion the aristocrat took the task upon himself. What methods he employed have never been revealed, though a combination of weights and wall-bars are rumoured. Suffice it to say that they proved ineffective in lengthening the gas man, though they did leave him with a nervous disposition and a solid commitment to the tenets of international Marxism.

Whether all this was known to Scamp I am not sure. Even if it had been, I don't believe he would have acted any differently. He was not the sort to make allowances. He had suffered and now it was someone else's turn. He waited until the little gas man was fully occupied on the cellar steps with torch and notebook then launched a frenzied assault upon his ankles, shredding his trouser turn-ups so completely they ended up looking like the sort of fringed bell-bottoms once favoured by Sonny and Cher.

The aunts offered no sympathy. In fact, they sent the poor fellow away with a flea in his ear. 'Imagine,' they later exclaimed indignantly to my mother, 'hopping around and yelling like that. No wonder Scamp got excited.'

'Scamp is very highly strung,' the youngest sister, Ethel, used to say.

'He bloody ought to be,' my granddad muttered. My granddad had not much time for his sisters, I should add.

'Ethel and Edna are here,' my mother would call on Christmas morning when he returned from one of the numerous walks he took the dogs on over the festive season.

'Oh, aye,' my granddad would reply. 'I thought they must be their broomsticks parked in the yard.'

Scamp ruled the sisters' household like an Ottoman emperor. Once, the doctor had come to visit one of the sisters that was sick. The sisters were often sick. Illness was their hobby. It was diverse, fascinating and cheap. This day the doctor left his brand new homburg on the table in the hall. When he came back, he found that Scamp had pulled it down and ripped it to shreds. The doctor was angry, the sisters horrified. 'Fancy that,' they said in outrage. 'A man of his education leaving his hat where a dog could get at it.'

The sisters were elderly and wild-looking, with skin the texture of worn suede. When they laughed it came out as a strange rattling hiss like the sound of a vacuum cleaner sucking up tacks. They lived in one of the ironstone mining villages of East Cleveland – isolated communities on the edge of the North Yorkshire Moors. Weird places. The nearest thing Britain has to the Appalachians. Walk down the streets of Boosebeck or Lingdale and you can almost hear the banjos twanging.

Once I worked in a pub in Guisborough, just on the fringes of the Moors. The pub had a function room and a '50/50' dance on Saturday nights. One week, the regular band couldn't play so the owner hired a piano-player on the recommendation of his window cleaner.

The piano-player had greasy hair, a vulpine face and a

dinner jacket so baggy it looked as if it had been designed
to be worn over a rucksack. Febrile menace flickered in his
red-rimmed eyes. He played well enough at first, plinking
and plonking through 'The Saint Bernard Waltz' and
'The Dashing White Sergeant'. Then an ageing teddy
boy's moll with backcombed hair the texture of loft insulation requested some rock 'n' roll. The pianist launched
into 'Great Balls of Fire'. By the time he reached the
second chorus he was on his feet, pounding the keys with
his fists and baying like a staghound. I'm not sure how
they calmed him down – in my mind I have an image of
the owner and a posse of waitresses hosing his crotch with
soda siphons – but the fact is that even now, thirty years
later, the memory of the incident still sends a shiver down
my spine. The howling pianist came from East Cleveland.

The sisters dressed in dark clothes and had powerful
religious beliefs based on a mixture of the Old Testament,
spiritualism and strong drink. It was the middle one of the
trinity that held the greatest sway. The East Cleveland
sisters had seances, Ouija boards, tarot cards and crystal
balls. Ethel painted pictures in garish acrylics having been
advised to take up art by an American Indian spirit. Edna
refused to countenance rail travel after a warning from the
beyond. 'Naruka saw me dead, in a tunnel surrounded
by steam,' she announced one day when we were round at
my great-grandmother's. 'Naruka was Cleopatra's hand-
maiden, so she has a feeling for temporal foreboding.'

The sisters' superstitions were a cause of some mirth in
the family, but the giggling had a nervous edge to it. 'You'll
be laughing on the other sides of your faces,' my granddad used to say, 'when they whistle up those flying
monkeys.'

Once, the phone rang at home and when my mother

answered it the voice of the eldest of the East Cleveland sisters asked, 'Did you know young Bobby Garbutt has passed over?'

My mother said she didn't, which was hardly surprising really as she hadn't a clue who young Bobby Garbutt was.

'Well,' the East Cleveland sister said, 'to be honest I only found out myself this morning. When I woke up there he was, standing at the foot of my bed, ashen in hue and asking why I hadn't been at his funeral.'

Afterwards my mother had to have a big glass of Scotch to settle her nerves.

The East Cleveland sisters made their own drink. Their speciality was cold tea wine. They brewed this ferocious concoction in a tin bath out in a shed. It proved to be Scamp's downfall. One day they left the shed door ajar and he got in and helped himself to several greedy mouthfuls.

Afterwards he staggered out into the backyard. There he saw what – in his drunken state – he thought was a mouse disappearing up the down pipe from the bathroom. He dived after it and got his head stuck fast. He wriggled and tugged but could not get free. Unfortunately for him, shortly afterwards one of the sisters pulled the plug out of the bath. Scampi was drowned.

'In a tunnel, surrounded by steam,' Edna said with wonder that Christmas. 'He was sitting on my lap when Naruka spoke to me. She must have got our auras muddled.'

On the radio programme *Desert Island Discs* many years ago, the distinguished jockey Lord Oaksey told Sue Lawley that his greatest regret was that he outlived so many dogs. I am not usually a sentimental type but I am with His Lordship on this one. Certainly, the memory of

Scamp and his sharp little teeth that overwhelms me each Christmas rarely fails to bring a tear to my eye.

The farmer had let the sheep into the turnip field. The sheep loved the purple-skinned swedes. You could hear them munching greedily away when they were first let loose among them. Four or so hours later, you couldn't hear the munching any more. This was not because the sheep had stopped eating. It was because the sound of munching was being drowned out by another noise. The root veg had a traumatic effect on the flock's digestive systems. Walking past the field was like listening to a bawdy and unrehearsed ovine version of the Frog Chorus. 'Maaah-parp,' it went. 'Toot-purp-baah, mair-maaaair-braaaaaaaarp, trurrrrp-maah.' After a week there was so much methane hovering over the field that a stray spark could have caused a firestorm. Heaven knows what it was doing to the planet. The sheep were emitting more greenhouse gases than the US Army. Their carbon footprint was the size of Cyprus. 'Maaah-frrrrarp-puuuuursht-baah,' they went and, if you listened carefully, you could almost hear the icecaps melting. Still, if they were enjoying themselves . . .

Mr Fudgie said he had taken the pledge. 'No more alcohol for me,' he said. 'No, never again. I've had it with drinking.' Mr Fudgie had experienced his epiphany three days before. He had gone to a work Christmas do. The firm had hired a coach and gone to a pub over in the Lake District. 'Lovely place,' Mr Fudgie said. 'Very "olde worlde" and right on the shores of Coniston Water.' They had booked a meal but it had taken a while coming and in the time they were waiting for it Mr Fudgie had, by his own admission, 'sunk some stuff'. During the meal there had been wine of several types followed by malt whisky of several varieties. 'After my fifth one – I think it was a Glen Turret, or thereabouts,' Mr Fudgie said, 'I began to feel a little bit under the weather.' So he had decided to step out into the car park and take some fresh air. 'I went out by what I thought was the door we'd come in through, right?' Mr Fudgie said. 'And the cold night hit me and suddenly I was absolutely bloody reeling.' It had been raining, Mr Fudgie said, and the car park was glistering in the moonlight. 'I couldn't see the coach anywhere, which I thought was a bit odd, but I reckoned maybe the driver had nipped off somewhere else and would be coming back later,' he said. 'So I decided that until he returned I'd take a walk back and forward across the car park to sober myself up a bit,' Mr Fudgie said. And so off he set. 'Well, I'd gone about forty yards when I noticed something weird. I looked down, Harry, and the car park was melting, literally melting! I was sinking into it. It was already up to me knees. I tried to get out of it but the more I walked the more I sank. It was sucking me down like quicksand! "Help!" I yelled, "Help! The car park's swallowing me! It's swallowing me!" I heard doors banging and people shouting and then . . . giggling.' Mr Fudgie shook his head glumly, 'I'd not gone out the door we'd come in through at all, had I? I'd gone out through the front door. I wasn't in the car park, I was in the bloody lake!' Mr Fudgie sighed, 'One more Scotch and I'd have drowned,' he said.

Snow had fallen heavily all day and then frozen overnight. Little Man and I towed Maisie and a friend of hers on their sledges to the nearest hill so they could go tobogganing. Little Man, it should be said, was not much help.

The dog is no Malamute. He is far too interested in smells. If Nanook of the North had had PBGVs pulling his sled instead of huskies he'd have gone round and round in circles for several hours before disappearing down a rabbit hole.

Nor did Little Man seem particularly excited by the snow. Ingemar had loved it. When snow fell, he would bound out of the door and run about with his snout stuck into it until a little pyramid of crystal flakes had formed on his nose. Then he'd flick the little white pile up into the air, jump and try to catch it. Sometimes it seemed like you could almost hear him chuckling.

Ingo's taste for snow was not so surprising when you considered his ancestry. Like schnauzers everywhere in those days, he had a docked tail. If his tail hadn't been docked it would have been curly. Schnauzers are part of the spitz family and spitz are northern dogs.

My dad and I once met a man with an Akita. Like all snow dogs, the Akita had a broad smiley face brimming over with joy and affection, combined with the intense eyes of a gun-slinger. This, you felt, was a nice dog, but not one you would like to see when it was angry. The man said his dog, Shoji, was a proper Akita: 'A lot of the ones you see about in Britain come from the US,' he said proudly. 'But this lad came from Japan.' The man said that the Akitas from Hokkaido Island had a much thicker coat than the dogs that came from America. 'He'll lie by the fire and he'll smell his fur singeing before he feels it,' the man said. And when it snowed, well, you couldn't get him to come in the house. 'He just sits out in the garden looking up at it falling from the sky like he's waiting to greet a long lost friend,' the man said.

Looking at Manny trudging through the snow I could

see why he might not care for it. As well as being from a southern clime he was also hardly built for the conditions. His legs were too short, his belly too low. As I watched him standing in the church field I was reminded of one of my grandfather's favourite jokes: a St Bernard and a dachshund are walking through the snow. The St Bernard says, 'My feet are cold.' And the dachshund replies, 'Your *feet* are cold.'

We left Maisie and her friend to have their fun. There were lots of kids on the slopes, a number of the boys engaged in that popular British winter pursuit of sign luge (or 'sluge' as it is known to aficionados). This is an exciting home-grown answer to the winter biathlon that culminates in competitors descending a grassy knoll on one of those striped plastic bars local councils use to fence off holes in the road. First, however, the slugers must locate a suitable bar using their skill, judgement and bits of information passed on by 'that fat kid whose granddad works on the bins'.

Next they steal the sign and smuggle it to the downhill course, evading police patrols and council workmen, and stopping every kilometre to let off a volley of abuse at anybody who asks, 'And where d'you think you're off to with that, you little hooligan?' Time deductions are awarded for accuracy and the closeness of F-word clusters (or 'Ramseys' as they are known to the sluge fraternity). But at least it keeps them out of mischief.

Snow began to fall again as Manny and I walked away. Down along the river there was nobody around. The snow lay thick on the ground and it kept on falling. Manny and I walked the length of the long field between the river and the railway line. No trains passed. The road above the line was deserted. A herd of beef steers on the other side

of the river chewed straw, the snow forming into low piles
on the bits of their hide where the fur was thick enough to
stop their body heat escaping. The water rolled past,
brown and heaving, tree trunks bobbing and spinning on
the surface. A couple of mallards whizzed by, like children
on a fairground ride. By the time we turned to walk back
across the field our footprints were almost totally filled in.
'It's like we've never been here at all,' I said to Manny.

We struggled up the road and, as we got to the wood at
the bottom of the garden, a badger suddenly jumped
through a gap in the wall and waddled across the snow in
front of us. The badger was a large male. As he walked
you could see the rolls of muscle rippling beneath the
dirty, creamy fur on his back. He scrambled up the bank
of the other side of the lane and disappeared through a
hole in the hedge. I looked down at Little Man. I'd
expected a yelp and a mad tugging on the lead, but
Manny was staring straight ahead at some fixed point further up the road. It was like he'd never seen the badger at
all, or smelled it either.

That night there was a heavy frost. When we went out in
the morning the snow crunched beneath our feet and
Manny did some impressive 'paw-spinning' on the ice in the
back lane, running on the spot for several seconds before
glancing down at the ground to see why he wasn't getting nearer to the elder tree he was aiming at. The sun was
coming up over the Bronze Age hill-fort to the east, dyeing
the sky cherry-pink. 'Red sky at night: shepherd's delight,'
I said to Manny, 'Red sky in the morning: shepherd's breakfast is on fire.' He didn't laugh. He'd heard it before.

As we walked past the gap in the wall where the badger
had appeared the previous day a black-and-white head
suddenly poked out between the stones, turned and

looked directly at us. I stopped dead in my tracks. The badger looked me up and down and then withdrew. When I looked down at Manny he was busy sniffing at a fallen branch. He appeared to have noticed nothing at all. At first I wondered if there was something the matter with his senses, if the cold weather had deadened them. When I considered it, however, I could see that there was nothing wrong with him at all. It was just that on this occasion the sense that was strongest was the sense of self-preservation. The badger was large and ferocious, with powerful claws and forelegs that could easily rip a dog's throat out.

Manny knew he was supposed to hunt, but he also knew he didn't want to. So he decided not to notice the badger. Like an office worker pretending they deeply respect the boss who bullies them, Manny was doing his best to save face.

The taxi driver was a big man who didn't so much sit in his Nissan Primera as wear it like an overcoat. A plasterer's cap was permanently affixed to his head and from beneath it wild and wiry hair stuck out at all angles like stuffing escaping from a sofa. Mirrored shades, a Zapata moustache and a voice that reverberated like an underground explosion were other characteristics. I had taken many journeys with this taxi driver over the preceding decade and was fully aware that his working day was made up of one long conversation that started the minute he turned the ignition and continued throughout his shift, regardless of the constant changes of passengers in the back of the vehicle. '. . . for fifteen year she was my faithful companion,' he rumbled as I slid onto the blue velour zebra-striped rear-seat and inhaled that unmistakable minicab smell of fresh mountain pine, king-size and take-aways. 'Never let me down. Good days and bad days, it didn't matter. When I got home she'd always be there waiting to lick my face.'

I judged from this that he was talking about a dog, but I didn't jump in immediately, because I couldn't yet entirely rule out a very enthusiastic and unusual wife – the taxi driver was from Tow Law, after all. 'Oh aye, you get used to having them around. The house feels empty without her. But I'll tell you something – of an evening, when I'm sat in front of the fire, I can still feel her lying against my leg. Or I open the front door and I'm sure that as I go to go out something brushes against me. There's definitely a presence,' he said.

'Sounds a bit mental, doesn't it?' he continued. 'Now, I'd have said the same myself one time. But after a few weeks of these feelings I went down to see the vet. He'd treated her all the time I'd had her, that fella. And I told him about feeling her in the room. And what he said was, he said, "That often happens. But only if they've had a happy life." So, you see, that's from a medical perspective,' the taxi driver said.

I wasn't sure how good the vet was with animals, but he was clearly a master of human psychology. 'Have you still got your dog?' the taxi driver asked. Once we'd been up to Dumfries and Galloway on holiday and I'd had to come home early, so I'd left Catherine and Maisie in Rockcliffe and Ingo and I caught the Girvan flyer back to Hexham where the taxi driver had given us a lift. I told him that Ingo had died.

'Aw, hey, I'm sorry to hear that,' the taxi driver said. 'He was a canny old lad. Sat at your feet in the front here. Looked like a big grey bear. What happened?'

What happened was that Ingo got old. He gradually
slowed up and then the power in his back legs went, so he
could no longer vault over stiles but instead had to squeeze
himself underneath them. Sometimes he got stuck and
I had to haul him through. He was a proud fellow and
it was plain from the look on his face that it wounded
his dignity. He got cataracts and he got tired. During the
day he lay on a thick clippy mat next to the radiator in my
office and slept so soundly and so quietly that sometimes
I'd bend down and put my hand on his chest to check that
he hadn't died.

Ingo got a cough. It was high summer and we thought
maybe it was just dust and pollen. We took him to the vet,
who gave him antihistamines. A week later we took Ingo
for a walk in the Lake District. He was still coughing but
he trotted around in the woods up above Staveley happily
enough. On the way back in the car he coughed even
more and we decided to take him back to the vet.
Catherine took him in and came back without him. 'They
say his right lung has filled with liquid. They need to do
some tests. We can pick him up tomorrow,' and then she
burst into tears. 'I hate it when they take him away,' she
said. 'He always goes along with the assistant so happily
and then, just when she opens the door through to the
back, he suddenly looks round to see where you are . . .'
And I knew exactly what she meant because we had seen
him do it many times. 'I don't want him to die in there,'
Catherine said.

He didn't. He came home the next day but he had been
probed and prodded and pumped full of antibiotics and
now he was incapable of walking even to the bottom of
the garden. We went back to the vet's every other day for
two weeks. He had more tests and more tablets. He started

to cough up blood. One hot Friday evening, he got up from his bed and walked very slowly into the hall and keeled over. He rallied briefly, was well enough an hour later to eat a couple of cold sausages that were left over from supper, but then he collapsed again. We sat up with him all night, listening to him sucking in air in big, wheezing, hardworking breaths, then, as dawn was breaking, he stopped making any sound at all.

'He got some sort of lung complaint,' I said to the taxi driver.

'What did they say at the vet's?'

'That'll be £629.17, please,' I said. The taxi driver chuckled.

'Aye, that'd be a vet,' he said.

'I had to pay in instalments,' I said.

'I tell you what, right?' he said after a moment's quiet contemplation. 'When you see what you pay to keep a dog well it makes you glad we've got a National Health Service for people, doesn't it?'

We buried Ingo at the bottom of the garden, put a big flat slab of stone over the plot and edged it with cobbles. It had been Maisie's birthday earlier in the week and she was having fifteen friends over for a party later that day. So I dug a grave in the morning and blew up balloons in the afternoon. And that, if you're lucky, is life.

Afterword

'A home without a dog never seems so peaceful, you know what I'm saying?' the taxi driver said. I replied that I knew exactly what he meant. A dog only relaxes when it is happy; fed, exercised, warm and free of fear.

On that first day Little Man came to live with us he battled desperately to prevent himself from nodding off. Whenever his eyelids began to fall he'd jump to attention and begin pacing around. For weeks afterwards, even when he slept, he kept his eyes open, the pupils rolling up into his head, the white filling the sockets and making him look like one of the living dead. In those weeks, he slept lying on his front, head between his paws, so that he could leap to his feet as fast as possible. Even in sleep, he was poised on the point of action, ready to fight or flee.

One morning in early June, when Manny had been with us for nearly three months, I looked across from my desk and saw that he had found a spot on the carpet that had been warmed by the summer sun. He was lying on his side but, as I watched, he hutched his bottom to the left and right so that he flipped over onto his back. And there he lay, in the sunshine with his legs flopping and his head tilted back exposing his throat, certain at last that he was in no danger, that life was good.

I watched Little Man lying there. His breathing was slow, each soft exhalation a sign of his contentment and with every breath that contentment spread further through the house.

Now you can order superb titles directly from Abacus

☐	The Far Corner	Harry Pearson	£7.99
☐	Racing Pigs and Giant Marrows	Harry Pearson	£6.99
☐	A Tall Man in a Low Land	Harry Pearson	£7.99
☐	Around the World by Mouse	Harry Pearson	£9.99
☐	Achtung Schweinehund!	Harry Pearson	£7.99
☐	Dribble!	Harry Pearson	£9.99

The prices shown above are correct at time of going to press. However, the publishers reserve the right to increase prices on covers from those previously advertised, without further notice.

──────────────── ⬭ ABACUS ⬭ ────────────────

Please allow for postage and packing: **Free UK delivery.**
Europe: add 25% of retail price; Rest of World: 45% of retail price.

To order any of the above or any other Abacus titles, please call our credit card orderline or fill in this coupon and send/fax it to:

Abacus, PO Box 121, Kettering, Northants NN14 4ZQ
Fax: 01832 733076   Tel: 01832 737526
Email: aspenhouse@FSBDial.co.uk

☐ I enclose a UK bank cheque made payable to Abacus for £ . . . .
☐ Please charge £ . . . . . . to my Visa/Delta/Maestro

Expiry Date ☐☐☐☐   Maestro Issue No. ☐☐

NAME (BLOCK LETTERS please) . . . .

ADDRESS . . . .

. . . .

. . . .

Postcode . . . . Telephone . . . .

Signature . . . .

Please allow 28 days for delivery within the UK. Offer subject to price and availability.